GRANDMA ROSE'S BOOK OF SINFULLY DELICIOUS

CAKES, COOKIES, PIES, CHEESE CAKES, CAKE ROLLS & PASTRIES

VINTAGE BOOKS

A DIVISION OF
RANDOM HOUSE
NEW YORK

GRANDMA ROSE'S BOOK OF SINFULLY DELICIOUS CAKES, COOKIES, PIES, CHEESE CAKES, CAKE ROLLS & PASTRIES

ROSE NAFTALIN

FIRST VINTAGE BOOKS EDITION, November 1987

Copyright © 1975 by Rose Naftalin

All rights reserved under International and Pan-American Copyright Conventions. Published in the United States by Random House, Inc., New York, and simultaneously in Canada by Random House of Canada Limited, Toronto. Originally published, in hardcover, by Random House, Inc., in 1975.

Library of Congress Cataloging-in-Publication Data
Naftalin, Rose.
Grandma Rose's book of sinfully delicious cakes, cookies, pies, cheese cakes, cake rolls & pastries.
Reprint. Originally published: New York: Random House, 1975.
Includes index.
1. Desserts.   2. Cake.   3. Cookies.   I. Title.
[TX773.N29   1987]   641.8'65   87-40077
ISBN 0-394-74671-6 (pbk.)

Manufactured in the United States of America
10   9   8   7   6   5   4   3   2   1

This book is dedicated to
Mrs. Davida Rosenbaum and her sons,
Richard, James, Howard and Kenneth,
and to
Mr. Bernard Naftalin and his daughters,
Lorie Ann and Nancy.
And a special dedication to my late grandson
William Michael Naftalin.
Once, when I asked him to take the garbage out,
he said,
"Grandma, even your garbage smells delicious."

CONTENTS

GRANDMA ROSE'S BOOK OF SINFULLY DELICIOUS

CAKES, COOKIES, PIES, CHEESE CAKES, CAKE ROLLS & PASTRIES

I was born in Russia, and at the age of five I came to America with my parents, a younger sister and a younger brother. We settled in Chicago, but in just two years, my father passed away, leaving my mother, who was then only twenty-nine, a widow with three small children.

After I graduated from elementary school, I went to a business college and took a course in English, typing and shorthand. My first job was as a secretary with an automotive manufacturing company, and while I was working to help support the family I finished my high school courses at night school. I kept busy during these years, but I always hoped I would accomplish something worthwhile in the end.

At the age of eighteen I met my husband and after a year's courtship we were married. I knew nothing about homemaking and had never baked or cooked in my life. I was terrified. I dreaded the dawn of each day because my husband was a man who appreciated fine foods. I went through a terrible struggle, but I made up my mind that since I had assumed these responsibilities I was going to make the best of it. I remember that one of the first things I asked my husband after we were married was, "How will I know a bad egg when I come across one?" He responded, "Don't worry, it will let you know."

I bought books, I talked to friends and I started looking for correspondence cooking schools. I also started going to a cooking school in Chicago and there I met someone who became a dear friend—Nanny Wolfe, who came from Vienna. It was as if God had sent her to me, because it was Nanny who taught me the fundamentals of baking. I had many failures before I learned. We were very poor and the expense of those failures was considerable, but my husband gave me a lot of encouragement and the incentive to go on.

My husband was an accountant, but when the Depression came he lost his job, and we moved to Toledo, Ohio, where he had heard of another position. By then I had two children and was baking as much as I could. I seem to have shown some talent because at a food fair I entered a coffee cake and won first prize—a handsome dining-room table and chairs—and I was very excited. The following year a fair was being held for all of Ohio and Michigan and I entered a sixteen-layer chocolate cream cake—taught to me by my Viennese teacher—and again I won first place.

Well, my husband's job didn't work out and we decided to buy a little delicatessen in our neighborhood that was for sale for practically no money. The kitchen consisted of a one-burner stove and we used to boil corned beef and other food back at our apartment. I would bake all the pastries at home and we would carry them to the delicatessen as they were finished. It was very hard. We worked in shifts until one in the morning when I would go home, set the yeast dough, and while it was rising, make cupcakes, ice a sheet cake, bake a batch of cookies and then roll the schnecken—cinnamon rolls—to let them rise again. I would stick another batch of cookies in the oven, and by that time the yeast dough would be ready to bake. So each day went in a terrible struggle to survive.

When my daughter, Davida, was nineteen years old and my son, Bud, was fourteen, my husband died. I kept the delicatessen, by then called Rose's Food Shoppe, and worked through the years to send my daughter through college and my son through engineering school.

My son and daughter eventually settled in Portland, Oregon, and I was lonely for them. I moved to Portland and opened a restaurant that later became quite famous. There, too, I worked twenty hours a day to keep up, doing all the baking and most of the cooking. People came from all over the United States to eat the baked goods, and we had orders pouring in from Maine to Alaska. Some of our customers would send specially designed boxes to ship the pastries back and forth in, and no one could believe that only one person produced all those pastries.

By the end of ten years I realized that my feet were slowly giving out, and with tears in my eyes, I sold the business. Then I decided that since I had been silent about my recipes for all those years, though people would always ask me for them, it was time to write a cookbook.

In this book, I want to impress the beginner as well as the sophisticated baker that anybody can learn to do anything if you are really in earnest and make an honest effort. Sometimes you must work by trial and error, but if you follow the instructions very carefully, I don't believe you can miss. Remember that what you put in you take out. I always use butter and heavy cream and the very best ingredients I can buy. It takes a lot of effort to bake, and it's a pity to waste that effort on inferior-quality ingredients. I realize that in these difficult economic times it may not always be possible to use the best, but, once in a while, splurge and make these recipes with the original, rich ingredients instead of using cheaper substitutes, and you will find that you get exciting results. There is no satisfaction like trying something new and having it work out wonderfully well.

My family and friends and my customers from all over the country have been telling me for many years that my pastries and cakes are the best they've ever eaten anywhere in the world. I hope they're right, and if they are, you can get exactly the same results with the recipes that follow.

NOTES ON INGREDIENTS

The recipes throughout this book call for "sweet butter"; by this I mean the *unsalted butter* that is widely available commercially. In recipes that call for cocoa, I have found that a *Dutch process cocoa* guarantees the best flavor. Where a recipe calls only for greasing cake pans (rather than greasing *and* flouring them), I have found that a *non-stick vegetable-oil spray* works well and simplifies matters. In general, of course, the most important thing to remember is to *use the best ingredients available in order to get the best results.*

CAKES

SIMPLE CHOCOLATE CAKE

CAKE

½ cup sweet butter, softened
1¾ cups cake flour
2 teaspoons baking powder
½ teaspoon baking soda
1½ cups sugar
½ teaspoon salt

1 cup sour cream
3 eggs, separated
1 teaspoon vanilla
2 ounces unsweetened
   chocolate, melted

Preheat oven to 350°. Lightly flour a 9″ tube pan. Place butter in a bowl. Sift together the flour, baking powder, baking soda, sugar, and salt. Add to the butter. Add sour cream and mix until flour is just dampened. Beat in electric mixer at medium speed for 2 minutes.

Add the egg yolks, vanilla, and melted chocolate. Beat egg whites until stiff and fold into batter. Turn into tube pan and bake about 45 minutes. When cool, remove from pan.

FROSTING

½ cup melted sweet butter
1 cup light brown sugar

1⅓ cups shredded coconut
⅓ cup light cream

Combine all ingredients and let stand for 5 minutes. Spread over the top of the cake and place under broiler. Heat topping until lightly brown and bubbly; watch carefully so it doesn't burn. Let cool.

GLAZE

½ cup semisweet chocolate
   morsels

2 tablespoons light corn syrup
1 teaspoon water

Combine chocolate morsels and corn syrup with water in top of double boiler. Place over hot, not boiling, water until chocolate is melted and pour over the frosting.

OLD-FASHIONED CHOCOLATE CAKE

CAKE

4 eggs, separated
2 cups sugar
1 cup sweet butter
4 ounces unsweetened
   chocolate, melted
1 cup mashed potatoes
   (mashed potatoes left from
   previous day are O.K.
   to use)

2 cups all-purpose flour
½ teaspoon salt
2 teaspoons baking powder
⅔ cup sour cream
½ teaspoon baking soda
2 teaspoons vanilla
1 cup chopped pecans

Preheat oven to 350°. Grease and flour one 9″ tube pan or two 9″ layer-cake pans. Beat egg whites until stiff. Gradually add ½ cup sugar, 1 tablespoon at a time, and beat until stiff. Set aside. Cream butter with remaining sugar

10

until fluffy, and add egg yolks, cooled chocolate, and mashed potato. Sift flour with salt and baking powder. Add to batter. Mix sour cream with baking soda and vanilla. Add to batter with the pecans and then, lastly, fold in the whites. Bake in tube pan about 50 minutes, in layer pans about 35 minutes. When cooled, remove from pan or pans.

FROSTING

3 ounces unsweetened
* chocolate*
¾ cup heavy cream
¼ cup water

1 cup sugar
1 tablespoon light corn syrup
1 egg, slightly beaten
1 tablespoon vanilla

Combine chocolate, cream, water, sugar, and corn syrup. Stir over low heat until chocolate is melted and sugar is dissolved. Raise heat a little and cook without stirring for about 10 minutes or until mixture is thick enough so that a bit dropped into a cup of cold water forms a soft ball. Stir 2 or 3 tablespoons hot chocolate into beaten egg. Pour egg mixture back into remaining chocolate mixture, stirring briskly. Add vanilla. Cook, stirring constantly, over low heat a few more minutes until a little thicker. Let cool and frost the cake.

DEVIL'S FOOD CAKE

CAKE

½ cup sweet butter
1¼ cups sugar
2 eggs
6 tablespoons cocoa
2 cups sifted cake flour

1 teaspoon baking powder
1 teaspoon salt
1 cup sour cream
1 teaspoon baking soda
1 teaspoon vanilla

Preheat oven to 350°. Grease and flour two 9″ layer-cake pans. Cream together butter and sugar, and add eggs, one at a time, beating after each addition. Sift together cocoa, flour, baking powder, and salt. Add alternately with sour cream mixed with the baking soda to the creamed mixture. Add vanilla. Pour into cake pans and bake for 30 to 40 minutes. Let cool.

CHOCOLATE FROSTING

1½ cups sugar
½ cup water
1½ teaspoons vinegar
3 egg whites

⅛ teaspoon salt
1 teaspoon vanilla
2 tablespoons cocoa

Boil together sugar, water and vinegar to 238°, or until syrup spins a long thread dropped from tip of spoon. Beat egg whites until stiff, add syrup gradually, beating constantly until frosting holds shape. Add salt and vanilla. Fold in the cocoa just before spreading between layers and on top and sides of cake.

FRENCH CHOCOLATE CAKE

You can cut this recipe in half very satisfactorily.

CAKE

1 pound sweet butter	*½ teaspoon salt*
4 cups sugar	*3 teaspoons baking powder*
12 eggs	*1 pint sour cream*
4 cups cake flour	*1 teaspoon baking soda*
1 cup cocoa	*2 teaspoons vanilla*

Preheat oven to 375°. Thoroughly grease three 10″ layer-cake pans. Cream butter until fluffy. Add sugar and beat until creamy. Add eggs, one at a time, beating after each addition.

Sift flour with cocoa, salt, and baking powder. Add to butter-and-egg mixture alternately with sour cream to which baking soda has been added. Add vanilla. Place batter into cake pans and bake for 40 minutes. Remove from oven and let cool completely. Cut each layer across, making six layers from the three layers.

FROSTING

½ *pound sweet butter*　　　2 *teaspoons vanilla*
½ *pound vegetable shortening*　1 *cup cocoa*
3 *cups powdered sugar*　　½ *cup hot black coffee*
6 *eggs*　　　　　　　*Large pecan halves*
¼ *teaspoon salt*

Cream butter and vegetable shortening. Gradually add sugar. Add eggs, one at a time, beating constantly. Add salt, vanilla, and cocoa. Pour in black coffee a little at a time until the mixture has the right consistency for spreading.

Frost cake between layers and on top and sides. Scatter pecan halves on top.

CHOCOLATE CHIP CAKE

CAKE

2 *cups all-purpose flour*　　½ *cup sweet butter, softened*
1 *cup brown sugar*　　　½ *cup semisweet chocolate*
½ *cup granulated sugar*　　　*pieces, finely chopped*
3 *teaspoons baking powder*　2 *teaspoons vanilla*
1 *teaspoon salt*　　　　3 *eggs*
½ *teaspoon baking soda*　　1¼ *cups buttermilk*

Preheat oven to 350°. Grease and flour two 9″ layer-cake pans. Blend all ingredients in an electric mixer. Beat for 2 minutes. Scrape bowl well and again beat at high speed for 3 minutes. Pour into pans and bake for 40 minutes. Cool and remove from pans.

FROSTING

2 cups powdered sugar   ½ cup sweet butter
½ cup cocoa   2 eggs
2 tablespoons hot coffee   1 teaspoon vanilla

Beat all together.
    Spread between layers and on top and sides of the cake.

DUTCH MOCHA CHOCOLATE CAKE

CAKE

The texture of this cake is very delicate. I've had compliments galore on it.

3 cups sifted cake flour   1 cup hot coffee
1 teaspoon baking soda   1 cup sweet butter
½ teaspoon salt   1 cup sour cream
¾ cup cocoa   2 teaspoons vanilla
2¾ cups sugar   5 egg whites

Preheat oven to 350°. Thoroughly grease three 9″ layer-cake pans. Combine flour, baking soda, and salt, and sift 3 times. Combine cocoa, ½ cup of the sugar and hot coffee. Cool. Cream butter and 1½ cups sugar until light and fluffy. Add cocoa mixture, sour cream, and vanilla. Add flour mixture, stirring until smooth. Beat egg whites with the remaining sugar until stiff. Fold into the batter. Pour batter into pans and bake for 30 minutes. Cool and remove from pans.

FILLING

½ cup all-purpose flour
Dash of salt
½ cup sugar
1 cup hot milk

3 egg yolks
1 cup whipped cream
1 teaspoon vanilla

Mix flour, salt, and ¼ cup of the sugar. Stir in hot milk, and place in top of double boiler over boiling water. Cook until smooth and thickened, stirring constantly. Combine yolks with the remaining sugar; add to mixture, and continue cooking. Stir for 3 minutes more. Cool completely, then fold in the whipped cream and vanilla.

Spread the filling between cake layers.

RICH CHOCOLATE FROSTING

1⅔ cups powdered sugar
3 squares unsweetened
  chocolate, melted
⅛ teaspoon salt

1 tablespoon hot coffee
3 egg yolks
¼ cup sweet butter, softened
1 teaspoon vanilla

16

Sift sugar and add to melted chocolate. Add salt and coffee, and beat well. Add yolks, one at a time, beating well after each addition. Add butter and vanilla, and beat well.

Spread on sides and top of cake.

CHOCOLATE ALMOND CAKE

CAKE

This cake freezes beautifully, but if you freeze it, glaze after removing from the freezer.

1 cup sweet butter	2 cups ground blanched
1⅓ cups sugar	almonds
6 eggs	Grated rind of 1 orange
8 ounces semisweet	½ cup grated cake or bread
chocolate, melted	crumbs

Preheat oven to 375°. Thoroughly grease and flour a 9″ tube pan. Cream butter with sugar. Add eggs, one at a time, beating hard after each addition. At this point the batter will look curdled but don't be alarmed. Stir in the melted chocolate, ground nuts, grated rind, and crumbs. Blend thoroughly and pour into pan. Bake for about 35 minutes. Touch to test if center is solid. Remove and cool cake completely.

GLAZE

4 ounces unsweetened chocolate	4 teaspoons honey
4 ounces semisweet chocolate	2 cups toasted blanched almond
4 tablespoons sweet butter	slivers

Combine chocolates, butter, and honey in the top of double boiler and melt over hot water. Remove from heat and beat until cool but still pourable.

Place the cake on a rack so the glaze runs evenly over the top and down the sides. Smooth the sides, and toss some toasted blanched almond slivers around the edge of the cake.

SIXTEEN-LAYER CHOCOLATE CREAM CAKE

This is an extravagant and difficult prize-winning cake that will lift everyone's spirits with its appearance and taste. Slice it thinly because it is very tall and solid.

CAKE

1 pound sweet butter	1 tablespoon orange brandy or
2 cups sugar	flavoring
12 eggs, separated	8 tablespoons cocoa
4 cups cake flour	6 tablespoons heavy cream or
½ teaspoon salt	sour cream
Grated orange rind	Powdered sugar

Preheat oven to 350°. Grease four 9″ cake pans. In a large bowl, cream the butter while gradually adding one cup of the sugar. Add egg yolks one by one, beating after each addition. Sift flour with salt and add to the butter mixture. Add orange rind and flavoring. Set aside.

Beat egg whites until quite stiff. Add the rest of the sugar, a tablespoon at a time, beating after each addition and continuing to beat until the whites form a stiff meringue. Fold the beaten whites very carefully into the flour mixture. Divide the batter in half and put it into two bowls. To one bowl, add the cocoa and cream.

Put 3 tablespoons of white batter in each of the four pans and with a spatula smooth the batter into as thin a layer as possible. Bake these four white layers for 15 minutes and turn out of the pans onto a cloth sprinkled with powdered sugar. Cover them with another cloth so they won't dry out. Make four more layers of white cake (you needn't wash and regrease the pans for the second baking). Turn them out and cover as before.

After finishing the white layers, wash and grease the pans. Bake eight thin layers of chocolate batter in two batches as above. While these are cooling, make the custard filling which will hold the layers together.

CUSTARD FILLING

1 pint cream (or half and half)	½ cup flour
6 egg yolks	½ pound sweet butter
½ cup sugar	2 teaspoons vanilla
¼ teaspoon salt	

Put all ingredients except butter and vanilla in the top of a double boiler and cook until thick. Pour the mixture into a bowl and gradually beat in the butter. Keep beating until creamy and cool. Add vanilla.

Stack the layers of cake, alternating white and chocolate, with a coating of custard between them. Leave top layer dry.

ICING

1 cup sweet butter	*2 teaspoons vanilla*
2 cups powdered sugar	*Dash of salt*
¾ cup cocoa	*2 tablespoons hot black coffee*
4 eggs	*Toasted almonds* (*optional*)

Cream the butter and gradually beat in the sugar, cocoa, eggs, vanilla, and salt. Beat until creamy and add coffee. Frost the sides and top of the cake. Decorate the top with toasted almonds if desired.

SWEDISH MOCHA CAKE

If you want to make this cake even richer, put a dollop of whipped cream on each square, but it's very good as it is.

2 cups strong coffee	*2 cups all-purpose flour*
2 cups granulated sugar	*½ teaspoon salt*
2 tablespoons cocoa	*½ teaspoon baking soda*
1 cup golden seedless raisins	*1 teaspoon cinnamon*
½ cup sweet butter	*1 teaspoon nutmeg*
½ teaspoon vanilla	*1 teaspoon ground cloves*
2 eggs	*Powdered sugar*

Preheat oven to 350°. Grease a 10" x 10" x 2" pan. Combine the coffee, 1 cup of the sugar, the cocoa, and raisins in a saucepan. Bring to a boil and simmer for about 15 minutes. Cool.

Cream the butter and add remaining sugar, gradually creaming until light and fluffy. Add vanilla. Add eggs, one at a time, beating after each addition. Mix and sift the remaining ingredients and stir into batter. Add the cooked mixture and bake about 1 hour. When cool, remove from pan. Place a paper lace doily on top of cake and shake powdered sugar over it. Carefully lift the doily and a design will appear. Cut in squares and serve.

WHITE BUTTER CAKE

The filling for this cake keeps indefinitely in the refrigerator, but if you're going to keep it, be sure to store in a plastic container covered with paper soaked in cognac.

CAKE

1 cup sweet butter	*¼ teaspoon salt*
2 cups sugar	*4 teaspoons baking powder*
8 egg whites	*1⅓ cups milk*
3 cups cake flour	*2 teaspoons vanilla*

Preheat oven to 350°. Thoroughly grease three 9" layer-cake pans. Cream butter and 1 cup sugar until light and fluffy. Beat egg whites until stiff and very gradually add the remaining sugar, 1 tablespoon at a time, beating constantly. Set aside. Sift the flour, salt, and baking powder together, and gradually add to the butter mixture alternately with the milk. Fold in the egg whites. Add vanilla. Put in pans and bake for about 35 minutes. Let cool.

FILLING

8 egg yolks
½ cup sugar
Juice and grated rind of
   2 large lemons

¼ cup sweet butter

In a heavy saucepan or the top of a double boiler, combine egg yolks and sugar over low heat. Add juice and grated rind of lemons. Stir, adding butter little by little. Cook until thick, stirring constantly.

Spread between the layers of the cake.

CHOCOLATE FROSTING

3 squares unsweetened
   chocolate
4 tablespoons sweet butter

2 cups powdered sugar
2 tablespoons light corn syrup
1 teaspoon vanilla

Melt chocolate with butter. Remove from heat and add sugar, corn syrup, and vanilla. If too thick, thin with a little black coffee to the right consistency.

Frost the top and sides of the cake.

WHITE LAYER CAKE WITH CHOCOLATE FROSTING

CAKE

⅔ cup sweet butter
1¾ cups sugar
3 cups cake flour
½ teaspoon salt
3½ teaspoons baking powder

1 cup milk
⅓ cup water
1 teaspoon vanilla
4 egg whites

Preheat oven to 350°. Grease three 9″ layer-cake pans. Beat butter until fluffy, add 1 cup of the sugar and continue beating. Sift flour with salt and baking powder, and add to butter mixture alternately with the combined milk and water. Add vanilla. Set aside. Beat egg whites until stiff. Very gradually add the remaining sugar and continue beating until stiff. Lastly, very carefully fold egg whites into the batter. Pour into pans and bake for about 30 minutes. Let cool.

CUSTARD FILLING

½ cup all-purpose flour
½ teaspoon salt
1 teaspoon vanilla
4 egg yolks

½ cup sugar
2 cups regular cream
1 cup heavy cream

Mix all ingredients except the heavy cream in the top of a double boiler. Cook until thick. Remove from heat and beat until cool. Beat cream until thick and fold into the cooled custard.

23

When cake layers are thoroughly cooled, remove from pans and spread the custard between them.

FROSTING

½ pound sweet butter	*2 teaspoons light corn syrup*
½ cup vegetable shortening	*½ cup cocoa*
2 eggs	*1 teaspoon vanilla*
2 cups powdered sugar	*2 cups toasted chopped almonds*

Beat together all ingredients except the almonds.

Spread over the top and sides of cake, and sprinkle with chopped almonds.

GRANDMA'S FAVORITE QUICK CAKE
(1 - 2 - 3 - 4 CAKE)

CAKE

1 cup sweet butter	*2 teaspoons baking powder*
2 cups sugar	*½ teaspoon salt*
4 eggs	*1 cup milk*
3 cups cake flour	*1 teaspoon vanilla*

Preheat oven to 350°. Grease three 9″ layer-cake pans. Cream butter and sugar until fluffy. Add eggs, one at a time, beating after each addition. Sift flour with baking powder and salt, and add to egg mixture alternately with the milk (begin and end with dry ingredients). Add vanilla. Pour into pans and bake for 30 minutes. Let cool completely.

CHOCOLATE ICING

3½ squares unsweetened
   chocolate
3½ cups sugar
1 cup milk

¼ cup light corn syrup
Pinch of salt
4 tablespoons sweet butter
1 teaspoon vanilla

Combine chocolate with sugar, milk, corn syrup, and salt. Boil in a large saucepan until candy thermometer registers 238°, or a soft ball forms in cold water. Remove from heat. Add butter and vanilla. Let mixture cool, then beat until creamy.

Spread between layers and on top and sides of the cake.

COMBINATION SPONGE AND POUND CAKE

½ cup whole blanched
   almonds
1 cup sweet butter
1 teaspoon vanilla
Grated rind of 2 lemons
Grated rind of 1 orange
4 eggs

4 egg yolks
1 cup sugar
1½ cups cake flour
2 tablespoons cornstarch
1 teaspoon baking powder
½ teaspoon salt

Preheat oven to 350°. Grease a 9″ Bundt kuchen pan and press almonds against sides and bottom.

Melt and cool the butter, then add vanilla and grated lemon and orange rind. In a large bowl combine eggs, egg yolks, and sugar. Beat for a minute, then set the bowl over a saucepan of hot water. Place saucepan over low heat for about 10 minutes, or until eggs are slightly warmer than lukewarm. *Do not let water boil.* Stir eggs occasionally to prevent them from cooking at the bottom of the bowl. When eggs are warm, remove from heat and beat until cool, thick and tripled in bulk. Sift flour, cornstarch, baking powder, and salt together, and fold gently into egg mixture, alternating with melted butter. Be careful *not* to overmix. Pour batter in pan and bake 45 minutes. Cool and remove from pan.

ORANGE BUTTER CAKE

CAKE

This cake is nice for a birthday. It makes 16 to 18 servings.

2 cups sweet butter	*½ teaspoon cream of tartar*
2 cups very-fine sugar	*4 cups cake flour*
10 eggs, separated	*½ teaspoon salt*
2 teaspoons vanilla	*1 teaspoon baking powder*
2 teaspoons orange liqueur	

Preheat oven to 325°. Thoroughly grease three 9″ layer-cake pans or one 9″ tube pan. Cream butter and 1 cup sugar until fluffy. Add yolks, one at a time, beating well after each addition. Beat in the vanilla and liqueur. In a separate bowl, beat whites until stiff, adding cream of tartar, and, very gradually, the remaining sugar, beating constantly until stiff. Mix the flour, salt, and baking powder. Gradually fold into butter mixture alternately with egg whites. Bake in layer pans for about 35 minutes; in a tube pan for 1½ hours. Let cool.

ORANGE FROSTING

½ cup sugar	1 tablespoon fresh orange juice
2 teaspoons light corn syrup	1 teaspoon grated orange rind
⅛ teaspoon cream of tartar	1 teaspoon orange flavoring
¼ cup water	¼ cup powdered sugar
1 egg white, stiffly beaten	

Place sugar, corn syrup, cream of tartar, and water in a small saucepan. Heat, stirring to dissolve the sugar. Use a brush to wash down the crystals from sides of pan. Cook syrup to 238° on candy thermometer, or until a soft ball forms when a spoonful is dropped into cold water. Gradually pour syrup on beaten egg white while continuing to beat. When frosting is thick, stir in the orange juice, rind, and flavoring. If the icing is too thin, thicken with powdered sugar.

Frost top and sides of cake baked in tube pan; for layer cake, frost also between layers.

ORANGE PECAN CAKE

This cake is nice served with sugared strawberries or fresh raspberries.

CAKE

¾ cup sweet butter, softened
¾ cup sugar
1 egg
1 cup all-purpose flour
½ teaspoon baking powder
½ teaspoon baking soda

½ teaspoon salt
½ cup buttermilk
Grated rind of 1 orange
⅓ cup chopped dates
½ cup pecan pieces

Preheat oven to 350°. Lightly grease and flour a 10" Kugelhupf pan. Cream together the butter and ½ cup sugar until light. Add the egg and beat until mixture is fluffy. Sift together the flour, baking powder, baking soda, and salt, and add, alternately with buttermilk, to the butter and egg mixture. Add grated orange rind, and fold in the dates and nuts to which 2 tablespoons flour have been added. Pour in pan and bake for about 50 minutes.

GLAZE

⅓ cup fresh orange juice
2 tablespoons orange liqueur

¼ cup granulated sugar
Confectioners' sugar

Mix orange juice, liqueur, and granulated sugar.

While the cake is still hot, prick it with a skewer at ½-inch intervals and slowly pour the orange mixture over it. Let the cake cool in the pan. Remove from pan and wrap in plastic bag and foil and let stand at room temperature for 2 or 3 days. Transfer cake to platter and dust with confectioners' sugar.

DANISH APPLE CAKE

CAKE

3 pounds cooking apples, cored, peeled, and cut into quarters
¼ cup water
⅔ cup sugar
Grated rind and juice of 1 orange
1 teaspoon vanilla

2 cups of fine bread or cake crumbs
1 teaspoon cinnamon
¼ cup brown sugar
½ cup plus 2 tablespoons sweet butter
1 jar raspberry jam

Preheat oven to 350°. Butter an 8″ baking pan which is 3″ deep. In a covered saucepan simmer the apples with water, sugar, orange rind, juice, and vanilla for about 25 minutes. Mash and set aside. Mix the crumbs, cinnamon, and brown sugar, and brown lightly in a skillet with 2 tablespoons of the butter.

Place a little of the crumb mixture on bottom of pan. Cover with a layer of the apple purée. Cover this with a layer of raspberry jam. Alternate crumbs, apples, and jam, finishing with a layer of the crumb mixture on top.

Using a large wooden spoon, press layers down firmly. Pour ½ cup melted butter over cake and bake for 40 minutes or until firm. Cool cake, unmold on a serving plate.

RED CURRANT GLAZE

⅔ cup red currant jelly　　　*Whipped cream*
2 tablespoons sherry

In a small saucepan, heat jelly with sherry. Cook, stirring, until jelly is melted and bubbling and coats spoon lightly.

Let glaze cool slightly before spreading with a pastry brush on top of the cake. Decorate with whipped cream.

APPLESAUCE CAKE

1 11-ounce box graham　　　　*1 14½-ounce can evaporated*
　crackers　　　　　　　　　　　*milk*
1½ teaspoons cinnamon　　　　*1 8-ounce can applesauce*
¾ cup sugar　　　　　　　　　　*1 teaspoon vanilla*
½ cup melted sweet butter　　*2 cups flour*
4 eggs, separated　　　　　　　*1 teaspoon baking powder*
3 tablespoons lemon juice　　*1 cup heavy cream, whipped*

Preheat oven to 350°. Grease and flour a 9″ spring-form pan. Crush crackers. Mix with cinnamon and 1 tablespoon of the sugar. Add melted butter and blend. Line bottom and sides of pan with cracker mixture, pressing firmly.

Beat yolks until thick. Add remaining sugar, lemon juice, milk, applesauce, and vanilla alternately with flour and baking powder. Beat egg whites until stiff and fold carefully into applesauce mixture. Pour into pan and bake 1 hour. Cool and top with whipped cream.

RASPBERRY CAKE

CAKE

½ cup sweet butter
¾ cup sugar
3 eggs

1 tablespoon orange juice
1 cup cake flour
⅛ teaspoon salt

Preheat oven to 300°. Butter and lightly flour an 8″ layer-cake pan. Cream butter with sugar until it is fluffy. Beat in eggs, one at a time, and also the orange juice. Gradually fold in the flour mixed with salt. Pour the batter into the pan and bake for 1¼ hours, or until a toothpick inserted in the center comes out clean. Let the cake cool in the pan for 10 minutes, then turn it out onto a wire rack to cool completely.

FILLING

1 10-ounce jar strained
raspberry preserves

2 pints fresh raspberries

Put a jelly roll pan under the wire rack and spread a thin layer of strained preserves on the top and sides of the cake. Cover the top with fresh raspberries.

TOPPING

1 envelope raspberry gelatin

1½ cups hot water

Arrange a 6″ wide band of waxed paper, doubled and lightly greased, around the cake. Fasten with tape or paper clip. Dissolve gelatin in hot water. When gelatin is syrupy carefully spoon a few tablespoons of it over the berries. Let gelatin set.

Spoon on the remaining raspberry gelatin and chill the cake for several hours. Remove the paper, cut cake into squares or diamond-shaped pieces and transfer to a serving plate.

LEMON CAKE

1 cup sweet butter	*½ teaspoon baking soda*
3 cups sugar	*1 cup sour cream*
5 eggs, separated	*Grated rind and juice of 1 lemon*
4 cups sifted all-purpose flour	*Powdered sugar*

Preheat oven to 325°. Grease and flour two 8″ x 5″ x 3″ loaf pans. Cream butter, adding 1½ cups of the sugar gradually, until light and fluffy. Beat the egg yolks and add to the mixture. Add the dry ingredients alternating with sour cream. Add juice and rind of lemon. Beat egg whites, gradually adding remaining sugar as you beat. When whites are stiff, fold into batter. Put in pans and bake 1 hour. Cool and remove from pans to serve. This cake requires no icing. Just sprinkle with powdered sugar when cool.

CARROT-PINEAPPLE CAKE

CAKE

1 cup sweet butter

2 cups sugar

3 eggs

2½ cups all-purpose flour

½ teaspoon salt

2 teaspoons cinnamon

2 teaspoons baking soda

2 teaspoons vanilla

1 cup grated raw carrots

1 cup drained crushed pineapple

1 cup dried shredded coconut

1 cup pecan pieces

Preheat oven to 325°. Grease a 9″ angel food cake pan. Cream butter with sugar and eggs. Sift together flour, salt, cinnamon, and baking soda and add gradually to butter-egg mixture. Add vanilla, carrots, pineapple, coconut, and nuts.

Pour into pan and bake for 1 hour and 15 minutes. Remove from oven, let rest for about 10 minutes.

SAUCE

2 tablespoons sweet butter

1 cup brown sugar

1 tablespoon light corn syrup

½ cup orange juice

1 teaspoon baking soda

½ cup sour cream

½ cup chopped pecans (optional)

Stir all ingredients except sour cream in a saucepan over low heat until dissolved. Let mixture come to a boil and cook for 5 minutes. Stir in sour cream.

Remove the warm cake from the pan and using a heavy fork, poke the top full of holes. Pour the hot sauce over the cake. If you wish, you can sprinkle the top with chopped nuts.

PINEAPPLE UPSIDE DOWN CAKE

¾ cup sweet butter

¾ cup brown sugar

3 slices of fresh pineapple,
    ½″ thick

¼ cup pecans (optional)

½ cup granulated sugar

2 eggs

½ teaspoon vanilla

1½ cups all-purpose flour

1½ teaspoons baking powder

½ teaspoon salt

½ cup milk

Sour cream

Preheat oven to 375°. Melt ¼ cup of the butter in a 9″ square pan. Also butter the sides of the pan. Sprinkle with brown sugar and arrange pineapple slices and nuts on top.

Cream the remaining butter with granulated sugar and beat in the eggs and vanilla. Sift together the flour, baking powder, and salt, and add to the egg mixture alternately with the milk. Spoon the batter carefully over the pineapple slices. Bake for about 35 minutes or until done. Let cake stand for 5 minutes before inverting on serving platter. Serve warm with sour cream.

SOUR CREAM FRESH BLUEBERRY CAKE

½ cup sweet butter, softened
1 cup granulated sugar
3 eggs
2 cups sifted all-purpose flour
½ teaspoon salt
1 teaspoon baking powder

1 teaspoon baking soda
1 cup sour cream
1 teaspoon vanilla
2 cups blueberries
½ cup brown sugar

Preheat oven to 325°. Thoroughly grease and flour an 8″ square pan. Cream butter and granulated sugar. Add eggs, one at a time, beating well after each addition. Sift dry ingredients and add gradually to the egg mixture alternately with sour cream, ending with flour mixture. Stir in the vanilla and 1 cup of the berries. Pour half the batter into the pan. Cover with remaining berries and sprinkle with brown sugar. Add remaining batter and bake for 45 to 50 minutes. Cool in pan 10 minutes. Remove to a wire rack to finish cooling.

BUTTERMILK SPICE CAKE

CAKE

2¼ cups cake flour

1 teaspoon baking powder

1 teaspoon salt

1 teaspoon cinnamon

¾ teaspoon baking soda

½ teaspoon ground cloves

¾ cup sweet butter

1 teaspoon vanilla

¾ cup brown sugar

1 cup granulated sugar

3 eggs

1 cup buttermilk

Preheat oven to 350°. Thoroughly grease two 9″ layer-cake pans. Sift together several times flour, baking powder, salt, cinnamon, baking soda, and cloves.

Cream butter with vanilla until fluffy. Gradually beat in brown sugar and white sugar and continue beating the mixture until very smooth and light. Add eggs, one at a time, beating hard after each addition.

Sift one-third of the flour mixture over the batter and stir it gently. Add buttermilk alternately with remaining flour mixture, ending with the last portion of flour.

Divide batter evenly between pans and bake for 30 to 35 minutes. Remove pans from oven and let the cake layers stand for about 5 minutes before turning them out onto wire racks to cool.

BOILED CARAMEL FROSTING

1½ cups brown sugar

½ cup water

½ teaspoon cream of tartar

6 egg whites

2 teaspoons vanilla or coffee
  extract

Put brown sugar, water, and cream of tartar in a deep saucepan. Stir the mixture over low heat until the sugar is dissolved. Raise the heat, cover the pan and bring the syrup to a boil over medium heat. Remove cover and boil until the syrup spins a long thread when dropped from a spoon or forms a soft ball in cold water, or until a candy thermometer registers about 238°. Beat egg whites until they are stiff enough to stand in peaks. Pour the syrup slowly in a thin stream into the egg whites while beating constantly with an electric beater until all the syrup has been added and the frosting stands in stiff peaks. Flavor the frosting with vanilla or coffee extract.

Spread between layers and on top and sides of cake.

MARBLE SPICE CAKE

This is a fine velvety, light, tender cake.

CAKE

1 cup sweet butter
2 cups sugar
4 eggs
3 cups sifted all-purpose flour
1 teaspoon salt
4 teaspoons baking powder

1⅓ cups milk
4 tablespoons cocoa
¾ cup nuts
2 teaspoons cinnamon
1 teaspoon ground cloves

Preheat oven to 350°. Thoroughly grease a 9″ or 10″ tube pan. Cream butter until fluffy, gradually adding 1½ cups sugar. Add eggs, one at a time, beating after each addition. Add flour, salt, and baking powder alternately with the milk. Spoon one-third of batter into pan. Mix cocoa, remaining sugar, nuts, and spices. Sprinkle half this mixture over batter in pan. Add another third of the batter, and then the rest of the cocoa mixture and finally the rest of the batter. Bake for about 1 hour. Let cool.

FROSTING

2 cups powdered sugar　　　*1 tablespoon light corn syrup*
½ cup cocoa　　　　　　　*4 tablespoons hot coffee*
4 tablespoons sweet butter

Stir all ingredients together and beat until mixture has the right consistency for spreading. If it's too thick, add more coffee; if too thin, add more powdered sugar.

Frost top and sides of cake.

FRUIT AND SPICE LAYER CAKE WITH
CREAM CHEESE FROSTING

CAKE

½ cup dried apricots
1 cup orange juice
½ cup sweet butter
1 cup sugar
2 eggs
2 cups sifted all-purpose flour
1 teaspoon baking powder
1 teaspoon baking soda
½ teaspoon salt

1½ teaspoons cinnamon
¾ teaspoon nutmeg
¾ teaspoon ground cloves
¾ teaspoon ginger
1½ cups buttermilk
1 cup cooked drained prunes,
  chopped
1 cup chopped pecans

Preheat oven to 350°. Butter two 8″ layer-cake pans.

Soak apricots in orange juice for 1 hour. Drain and purée with a little of the orange juice in the blender.

Cream butter and sugar. Beat in eggs until mixture is light. Sift all dry ingredients and add to butter mixture alternately with buttermilk. Stir in apricot purée, prunes and nuts and turn batter into pans. Bake for about 45 minutes. Let the cake layers cool in pans for 5 minutes and turn out on wire racks to cool completely.

CREAM CHEESE FROSTING

6 ounces cream cheese,
  softened
1 egg, separated

1 teaspoon vanilla
Pinch of salt
3 cups powdered sugar

In a bowl beat cream cheese until it is light. Beat in the egg yolk, vanilla, and salt. Gradually beat in the sugar until frosting is smooth. Whip the egg white until stiff and fold into the frosting.

Spread frosting between layers and on top and sides of cake. Wrap in plastic and foil and store in refrigerator for at least 2 days. Remove wrappings while cake is still cold and serve at room temperature.

DATE AND NUT CAKE

CAKE

1 cup chopped dates	*½ cup sweet butter*
1 cup water	*1½ cups sugar*
2½ cups cake flour	*3 eggs*
1 teaspoon baking powder	*1 cup chopped pecans*
1 teaspoon baking soda	*1 cup buttermilk*
1 teaspoon salt	*1 teaspoon vanilla*

Preheat oven to 325°. Grease well a 9″ tube pan. Cook dates and water in a saucepan until thick. Sift together flour, baking powder, baking soda and salt. Cream butter, gradually add sugar and continue beating until well blended. Add eggs, one at a time, beating after each addition. Add date mixture, pecans and dry ingredients alternately with buttermilk. Add vanilla. Pour into the pan and bake for about 1 hour. When partially cooled, remove from pan.

FROSTING

¾ cup chopped pecans

½ cup brown sugar

5 tablespoons sweet butter

3 tablespoons heavy cream

Combine all ingredients in a saucepan and cook over low heat for 3 minutes.
While frosting is still hot, spread it evenly on the top of the cake. Put the
cake 4 inches from a hot broiler for 2 minutes, watching carefully so it
doesn't burn. Transfer to a wire rack and let it cool.

PINEAPPLE NUT BREAD

3 cups all-purpose flour

2 teaspoons baking powder

½ teaspoon baking soda

1 teaspoon salt

½ cup sugar

1 cup raisins

½ cup chopped pecans

1 egg

1½ cups crushed pineapple,
   undrained

¼ cup melted sweet butter

1 teaspoon vanilla

Preheat oven to 350°. Grease 2 loaf pans. Sift flour with baking powder,
baking soda, salt, and sugar into large mixing bowl. Stir in raisins and nuts.
Beat egg and add pineapple, butter, and vanilla. Stir slowly into flour
mixture just until it is moistened. Pour batter into pan and bake for about 55
minutes. Cool thoroughly before slicing.

APPLE ORANGE NUT LOAF

CAKE

2 large oranges
1 cup golden seedless raisins
2 cups applesauce
4 cups sifted all-purpose flour
4 teaspoons baking powder
2 teaspoons baking soda

2 cups sugar
1½ teaspoons salt
1½ cups chopped pecans
2 eggs, slightly beaten
6 tablespoons melted sweet butter

Preheat oven to 350°. Grease two 8″ x 5″ x 3″ loaf pans. Squeeze oranges. Put the rinds and raisins through medium blade of food chopper. Add the juice, rind, and raisins to the applesauce. Sift together the flour, baking powder, baking soda, sugar, and salt. Add the applesauce mixture and nuts. Mix thoroughly, then add the eggs and melted butter. Pour batter into pans and bake for about 1 hour and 15 minutes. Remove cakes from pans and cool on wire rack before frosting. Let stand overnight before cutting.

OPTIONAL FROSTING

2 cups powdered sugar
Juice of 2 oranges

Juice of 1 lemon

Mix ingredients thoroughly and spread over loaves.
   You may sprinkle the cakes with powdered sugar instead of frosting them.

POUND CAKE

Traditionally pound cake is made with a pound each of the ingredients. This makes a fine-textured cake. The only leavening is provided by the stiffly beaten egg whites.

2 cups sweet butter	*1 teaspoon cream of tartar*
2 cups sugar	*2 cups chopped glazed fruits*
10 large eggs, separated	*2 teaspoons grated lemon rind*
1 teaspoon salt	*4 cups sifted all-purpose flour*

Preheat oven to 350°. Thoroughly grease and flour two 8″ x 5″ x 3″ loaf pans or one 9″ tube pan. Cream butter and 1¼ cups sugar until mixture is light and fluffy. Add egg yolks, one at a time, beating well after each addition. Add salt to egg whites and beat until they form stiff peaks. Add cream of tartar and the remaining sugar, 1 tablespoon at a time, beating well after each addition; continue to beat until egg whites are stiff. Combine the fruits with lemon rind and 4 tablespoons flour. Gently fold egg whites and remaining flour, alternately, into butter mixture. Fold in the fruits. Pour batter into prepared pans and bake until golden brown (in loaf pan about 1½ hours, in tube pan about 2 hours).

MOCHA-FLAVORED POUND CAKE

I know that the current trends in eating would not go along with the cup of butter that begins this recipe, but I always feel that if you're going to spend a lot of time baking you ought to use the best ingredients so the results will be worthwhile.

1 cup sweet butter	*½ teaspoon baking soda*
2 cups sugar	*½ cup cocoa*
4 eggs	*3 tablespoons instant coffee*
2¾ cups all-purpose flour	*1 cup sour cream*
½ teaspoon baking powder	*2 teaspoons vanilla*

Preheat oven to 325°. Grease one 10″ or 9″ angel food cake pan. Cream butter and sugar until smooth. Then beat in the eggs, one at a time, until well blended. Measure and sift together the flour, baking powder, baking soda, cocoa, and instant coffee. Add to butter mixture along with sour cream and vanilla and beat until well blended. Pour batter into pan and bake for about 1 hour and 30 minutes—a skewer inserted in center comes out clean when cake is done. Let stand in pan about 10 minutes, then invert onto wire rack, remove from pan and cool. To serve, cut in thin slices.

HAZELNUT CREAM CAKE

CAKE

This is one of my favorites.

3 cups heavy cream
6 large eggs
3 cups sugar
2 teaspoons vanilla
2 teaspoons orange flavoring

3 cups all-purpose flour
½ teaspoon salt
4 teaspoons baking powder
2 cups finely ground toasted
    hazelnuts

Preheat oven to 350°. Thoroughly grease and flour four 9″ layer-cake pans. Whip the cream, but not till it becomes very stiff, and set aside in refrigerator. Beat eggs until thick, gradually adding sugar. Add vanilla and orange flavoring. Sift flour with salt and baking powder and fold one-quarter of the flour mixture into the eggs. Mix remaining flour with ground nuts and fold into the egg batter alternately with the whipped cream, until all ingredients are incorporated. Pour batter into pans evenly. Bake for about 25 to 30 minutes. Remove from heat and let rest for about 10 minutes before removing from pan. Cool thoroughly.

BRANDY BUTTER FILLING

2 eggs
6 tablespoons cognac
8 tablespoons sweet butter
2 cups plus 4 tablespoons
    sugar

2 tablespoons cornstarch
About 2 cups apricot preserves
1½ cups finely ground toasted
    hazelnuts

Beat the eggs and add cognac, 4 tablespoons butter, 2 cups sugar, and corn-starch. Cook over moderate heat and simmer, stirring, for about 5 minutes. Remove from heat, add remaining butter and beat until smooth. As it cools, the filling will continue to thicken. When cake layers have cooled, spread the filling between them. Strain apricot preserves, add remaining sugar, and cook until thick, about 10 minutes. Paint the sides of the cake with this apricot glaze and then sprinkle the sides with hazelnuts. Work quickly because the glaze dries quickly.

ROYAL FROSTING

2 egg whites
1 teaspoon lemon juice
2 teaspoons cognac
Dash of salt

3 cups powdered sugar
1 semisweet chocolate bar
* (optional)*

Beat all ingredients until thick.

Frost top of cake and, if you wish, decorate with chocolate curls. I make curls by scraping a vegetable peeler down the chocolate bar.

CHOCOLATE CREAM CAKE

This is a miracle of a cake, made without flour. Everybody who loves to lick the batter bowl will love this cake, since it's iced with half the batter.

½ cup sugar
4 ounces sweet butter
4 squares semisweet chocolate,
  melted and cooled

8 eggs, separated
Some halved pecans

Preheat oven to 350°. Butter and lightly flour an 8″ square baking pan. Blend sugar with butter until the mixture is light and fluffy. Stir in the chocolate. Mix in the egg yolks, one at a time, beating well after each addition. Beat egg whites until stiff and very carefully fold them into the chocolate mixture.

Pour *half* of the batter into baking pan, set in oven and immediately reduce heat to 300°. Pour the remaining batter into a bowl, cover and refrigerate. Bake the cake for 45 minutes, or until a wooden toothpick inserted in the center comes out clean. Let the cake cool completely.

Spread half of the reserved batter over the cake and chill until set. Spread the remaining batter over it and chill overnight. Cut the cake into 16 squares. Put pecans on top to decorate.

LORD AND LADY BALTIMORE CAKE

This is really a union of two different cakes—one white and one yellow—but they must be prepared and baked separately. Start with the white.

CAKES

⅞ cup sweet butter, softened
1¾ cups fine granulated sugar
2 teaspoons vanilla
2 whole eggs, plus 2 egg
  whites

3 cups sifted cake flour
3½ teaspoons baking powder
½ teaspoon salt
⅞ cup milk

To prepare the white cake, preheat oven to 350°. Lightly butter and flour a 9″ layer-cake pan. In a mixing bowl cream together 6 tablespoons butter, ½ cup sugar and 1 teaspoon vanilla until the mixture is smooth and fluffy. In a separate bowl beat the egg whites to the soft peak stage, add ¼ cup sugar, a little at a time, continuing to beat until egg whites are stiff.

Sift together the flour, baking powder, and salt. Set half of the mixture aside (to be used for the yellow cake), and blend the remainder a little at a time into the butter mixture alternately with ½ cup milk, also added in small amounts.

Gently but thoroughly fold in the beaten egg whites. Spread the batter evenly in the pan. Bake for 25 minutes. Cool the cake for 5 minutes before turning it out onto a wire rack to complete cooling.

Prepare the yellow cake as follows. Increase oven heat to 375°. Lightly butter and flour a 9″ layer-cake pan. In a mixing bowl cream together the remaining butter, sugar, and vanilla, as you did for white cake. Vigorously beat in the whole eggs one at a time. Blend in the reserved flour mixture, a little at a time, alternately with the remaining milk, also added in small amounts. Spread the batter in the pan and bake for 25 minutes. Cool the cake as directed for the white.

LEMON MERINGUE ICING

1 whole lemon
2¼ cups sugar
3 egg whites
⅓ cup water
¼ teaspoon cream of tartar

2 tablespoons lemon juice
½ cup chopped raisins
½ cup chopped pecans
¼ cup chopped maraschino cherries

Peel lemon and set aside. Thoroughly rub the peel into the sugar. In the top of a 2-quart double boiler, combine the sugar, egg whites, water, cream of tartar, and lemon juice. Set the pan over boiling water and beat with a rotary beater or electric hand beater for 6 minutes, or until mixture flows from the withdrawn beater in ribbons that hold their shape on the surface. Remove the pan and continue beating until the meringue is firm enough to spread and has cooled completely. You will have about 3 cups. Transfer one-third of the icing to another bowl and blend into it the chopped raisins, pecans, and cherries.

Split the cooled cakes each into 2 layers. Spread the yellow layers and one of the white with the mixture. Reassemble the spread layers with the white one in the middle. Top with the uncoated white layer. Cover the top and sides of this four-layer cake with the remaining icing.

SOUR CREAM POUND CAKE

½ cup sweet butter, softened	1 cup sour cream
3 cups sugar	Grated rind of 1 lemon and
4 eggs	1 orange
3 cups sifted all-purpose flour	Juice of 1 lemon
½ teaspoon baking soda	2 teaspoons vanilla
½ teaspoon salt	4 tablespoons cinnamon

Preheat oven to 350°. Grease and flour a 10″ angel food cake pan. In a large mixing bowl beat the butter until creamy. Gradually add 2½ cups sugar, beating until mixture is light and fluffy. Beat eggs into mixture, one at a time, beating well after each addition. Sift flour again with soda and salt. Beat into butter mixture alternately with the sour cream mixed with lemon and orange rind, lemon juice, and vanilla (begin and end with dry ingredients).

Pour half the batter into pan. Sprinkle it with ¼ cup sugar mixed with 2 tablespoons cinnamon. Pour over this the remaining batter and sprinkle the remaining cinnamon and sugar on top. Bake for 1 hour.

Cool in pan for 10 minutes and turn out on a wire rack to cool completely.

FRUIT POUND CAKE

This cake keeps well and also freezes well.

4 cups sifted all-purpose flour	*1 pound sweet butter*
1 pound candied cherries	*1 pound powdered sugar*
1 pound candied diced	*12 eggs*
pineapple	*½ teaspoon salt*
Rind of 2 oranges, chopped	*1 teaspoon baking powder*
1 pound pecan pieces	*1 teaspoon brandy*

Preheat oven to 325°. Thoroughly grease a 10″ angel food cake pan or two 8″ x 5″ x 3″ loaf pans. Sift half the flour over the fruits and nuts. Set aside.

Cream butter with sugar and beat until light and fluffy. Add eggs, one at a time, beating after each addition. Add remaining flour sifted with salt and baking powder. Add brandy, fruits, and nuts, and pour in pan. Place baking pan in a pan of water and bake for about 2 hours.

ANGEL FOOD CAKE

Follow these instructions exactly. The result will delight you. This recipe is worth the price of the book.

CAKE

1½ cups sifted cake flour
2 cups extra-fine granulated
   sugar
2 cups egg whites (about
   14 eggs)

2 teaspoons cream of tartar
½ teaspoon salt
1 teaspoon vanilla

Preheat oven to 400°. Sift flour, add ³/₄ cup sugar, and sift the mixture 5 times. Beat egg whites until stiff. Add cream of tartar and salt, continue beating, and very gradually, 1 tablespoon at a time, beat in the remaining sugar. When batter looks shiny and stiff, very gradually fold in the sifted flour mixture and vanilla.

Pour batter into a 9″ angel food cake pan and bake for 10 minutes. Reduce heat to 350° and bake for 30 minutes. Reduce heat again to 300° and bake until cake is done, about 1 hour. Remove from oven, turn upside down to cool. When cold, remove from pan and frost or leave plain.

SUGGESTION FOR FROSTING (delicious)

1 6-ounce package strawberry
   jello
½ cup boiling water
2 cups marshmallows

1 quart washed and sugared
   in-season berries
1 pint whipping cream

Dissolve jello in the boiling water. Add marshmallows and stir until dissolved. When cooled and thickened, beat until fluffy. Add berries and fold in the cream. Spread evenly over cake.

FILLED ANGEL FOOD CAKE

1 Angel Food
   Cake (see above)
4 eggs
1½ cups sugar
¼ cup lemon juice

½ cup orange juice
1 teaspoon lemon rind
2 teaspoons orange rind
2 cups whipped cream
1 teaspoon vanilla

With a sharp knife carefully hollow out the cake leaving a shell about 1 inch thick. Cut the cake removed from the center into small pieces.

Beat eggs with 1 cup sugar. Add lemon and orange juices and rind. Cook and stir over hot water until very thick.

Chill. When cold, fold in 1 cup whipped cream and the cake pieces. Pour into the cake shell and chill until firm. Frost with the rest of the whipped cream to which remaining sugar and vanilla have been added.

CHOCOLATE ANGEL FOOD CAKE

CAKE

1 cup sifted cake flour

4 tablespoons cocoa

1⅓ cups sugar

⅛ teaspoon salt

11 egg whites

1 teaspoon cream of tartar

1 teaspoon vanilla

Preheat oven to 350°. Sift flour, cocoa, and ⅓ cup sugar five times. Add salt to egg whites and beat until stiff. Add cream of tartar to egg whites and then gradually, 1 tablespoon at a time, the balance of the sugar, beating until very stiff. Add vanilla. Fold in the flour mixture a little at a time. Pour batter into a 9" tube pan and bake for 15 minutes. Reduce heat to 300° to finish baking. Total baking time is about 1 hour.

CHOCOLATE MARSHMALLOW BUTTER CREAM FROSTING

2 egg whites

3 tablespoons water

1 teaspoon vanilla

¼ teaspoon cream of tartar

1 cup sugar

1 cup sweet butter

¼ cup sifted cocoa

⅛ teaspoon salt

Combine egg whites, water, vanilla, cream of tartar, and sugar in upper part of double boiler. Mix well, beat over heat until mixture stands up in peaks. If electric beater is used, bring water in lower part of double boiler to a rapid boil and beat for about 2 minutes. Remove from stove and beat 3 or 4 minutes at high speed until it stands in high peaks. Be careful not to scrape beater against bottom of pan as it will darken the mixture. Allow the mixture to cool, keeping it covered with a damp cloth to prevent a crust from forming.

Cream butter thoroughly and add the cold marshmallow mixture to it little by little, beating thoroughly. Add cocoa (use more cocoa if more intense flavor is desired) and salt. Have marshmallow mixture and butter at about same temperature and consistency before combining them (otherwise, frosting will have a tendency to separate or curdle). Keep cool, not cold. If frosting should curdle add about 2 tablespoons hot melted butter and beat well.

Frost top and sides of cake.

MANY, MANY LAYERS CAKE

CAKE

This cake is a beautiful and exciting masterpiece.

1⅔ cups all-purpose flour   *1 cup cold sweet butter*
¼ teaspoon salt   *4 tablespoons ice water*

Preheat oven to 450°. Grease the *back* of a 9″ layer-cake pan before each layer is baked. Sift flour and salt in a bowl. Cut butter in with either two knives or your fingertips until the mixture looks like coarse meal, then very gradually cut in the ice water. Cover and chill 30 minutes. Divide into 6 to 7 portions. Roll out each very thinly on waxed paper in 9″ circle, brush with ice water, and sprinkle with sugar. Bake on back of pan for 6 to 8 minutes, or until golden brown.

FILLING

1 tablespoon unflavored   ¼ cup maraschino cherry juice
  gelatin   1 can applesauce

Sprinkle gelatin on the cherry juice and place over hot water until thoroughly dissolved. Add to applesauce. When cold, use as filling on *every other* layer of cake. On alternate layers fill with the following:

CUSTARD FILLING

2 cups half-and-half cream   ½ cup all-purpose flour
4 egg yolks   1 cup whipped cream
½ cup sugar   1 teaspoon vanilla
Dash of salt

Heat half-and-half cream. Beat egg yolks with sugar, salt, and flour. Gradually add hot cream and cook in double boiler until thick. When cold, add whipped cream and vanilla, and stir.

    Spread on every other cake layer and assemble the cake.

TOPPING

1 cup heavy cream   Chopped toasted blanched
½ cup sugar   almonds

Whip cream and sugar.

    Frost sides and top of cake. Sprinkle entire cake with almonds. Put in refrigerator for 1 hour before serving.

MERINGUE-LAYERED NUT CAKE

CAKE

4 eggs, separated
4 tablespoons sugar
1 teaspoon vanilla
Pinch of salt

⅓ cup ground toasted almonds
2 tablespoons cake or bread
  crumbs
Rum

Preheat oven to 325°. Butter and lightly flour an 8" round cake pan. Beat egg yolks until frothy. Gradually add sugar and continue to beat until mixture forms ribbons when beater is lifted. Stir in the vanilla. In another bowl, beat egg whites with salt until stiff. Gently fold one-quarter of the egg whites into the yolk mixture. Pour the yolk mixture over the remaining egg whites and sprinkle with almonds and crumbs. Gently fold the mixture together until no traces of egg whites appear. Pour batter into pan and bake for about 50 minutes. Cool cake in pan for 20 minutes and then turn out on a wire rack.

MERINGUE

4 egg whites
Pinch of salt

½ cup plus 1 tablespoon sugar
½ cup ground toasted almonds

Let oven cool to 250°. Butter and flour 2 baking sheets. Beat egg whites with a pinch of salt, adding ½ cup sugar, a little at a time, while you continue to beat. Combine almonds with 1 tablespoon sugar and carefully fold into the meringue.

Draw an 8″ circle on each baking sheet. Fill a pastry bag fitted with a ½″ plain tube with the meringue and pipe 2 layers on the baking sheets starting from the edges of drawn circles and piping diminishing circles until the areas are filled. Smooth the top and bake for 45 minutes. Let cool and cover with the following:

MOCHA BUTTER CREAM

⅔ cup granulated sugar   1 cup sweet butter
½ teaspoon cream of tartar   1 tablespoon instant espresso
¼ cup water   2 tablespoons rum
4 egg yolks   Powdered sugar

In a small saucepan dissolve sugar and cream of tartar in water. Brush down any sugar that clings to sides of pan and cook syrup over high heat until it reaches the soft ball stage (238°) on thermometer. With an electric beater, beat 4 egg yolks until thick. Turn to high speed and pour in the hot syrup in a thin stream, continuing to beat until thick and cooled. Then beat in the butter, a little at a time. Dissolve espresso in 1 tablespoon rum and add it to the butter cream.

Split the cake in half horizontally and sprinkle each half with 1 tablespoon rum. Put 1 tablespoon butter cream in the center of an inverted cake pan and put one of the meringue layers on the tin (the butter cream will hold it down). Spread a thin layer of the butter cream over the meringue. Top it with one of the cake layers, cut side up, and spread it with some of the butter cream. Cover with the other cake layer, cut side down, and spread it with more of the butter cream. Put on the second layer of meringue, smooth side up With a spatula, spread some of the butter cream around the sides of the cake.

Sift powdered sugar on top. Fill a pastry bag fitted with a star tube with remaining butter cream and pipe rosettes around the top of the cake. When finished you will have two layers of meringue and two yellow layers combined with the butter cream.

AUSTRIAN LAYER CAKE

This cake is very rich, so a thin slice will go a long way. It keeps well in the refrigerator for days.

CAKE

6 tablespoons sweet butter, softened	1 cup all-purpose flour
1 cup sugar	¾ cup cornstarch
6 eggs	½ teaspoon salt
⅓ cup rum	2 teaspoons baking powder
	Rind of 2 lemons, grated

Preheat oven to 350°. Butter and flour a 9″ spring-form pan. Cream butter, add sugar gradually, beating after each addition. Beat in the eggs, one at a time. Add rum, flour—mixed with cornstarch, salt, and baking powder—and lemon rind. Pour into pan and bake for about 40 minutes. When cake is cooled, cut it into three layers.

FILLING AND FROSTING

1 cup sugar
3/4 cup water
1/4 teaspoon cream of tartar
10 egg yolks

1/4 cup rum
1 pound sweet butter, softened
1 cup red raspberry jam
1/2 cup chopped nuts

Boil sugar, water and cream of tartar until syrup reaches 238°, or a drop in cold water forms a soft ball. Beat yolks and very slowly pour the boiled syrup onto yolks while continuing to beat until thick. Add rum and gradually add butter while continuing to beat. Put mixture in refrigerator for about 1 hour.

Spread each cake layer with jam and then with frosting. Spread frosting on top and sides and sprinkle sides of cake with chopped nuts. Use pastry bag with star tube to decorate the top as you wish.

FRESH PLUM KUCHEN CRISP

CAKE

2 cups all-purpose flour
2 teaspoons baking powder
1/2 teaspoon baking soda
1/4 teaspoon salt
1 egg
1/3 cup sugar

3/4 cup sour cream
4 tablespoons melted sweet
    butter
18 large fresh plums or cooked
    prunes

Preheat oven to 425°. Thoroughly butter a 10″ x 14″ baking pan. Sift together flour, baking powder, baking soda, and salt. In a mixing bowl, beat egg slightly, beat in the sugar, add sour cream and melted butter. Add dry ingredients, stirring only long enough to moisten. Spoon into pan and press up against sides of pan. Cut plums or prunes in half, remove pits, and place cut side up over dough.

TOPPING

½ cup sweet butter
1 cup brown sugar
¾ cup all-purpose flour
¼ teaspoon ground cloves

1 teaspoon cinnamon
1 pint sour cream (optional)
1 cup heavy cream (optional)

Melt butter. Remove from heat and stir in the brown sugar, flour, cloves, and cinnamon.

Sprinkle over plums or prunes and bake immediately just until dough is set and fruit is tender.

Serve either plain as coffee cake or as dessert topped with sour cream (at room temperature) mixed with 1 cup heavy cream.

FRESH PINEAPPLE SAVARIN

This method of putting a yeast cake together is different and very interesting. It does take quite a bit of effort but the result is so unusual that I think you'll enjoy serving this.

CAKE

3 cups cake flour
2 yeast cakes
¼ cup warm water
3 eggs

5 teaspoons sugar
1 teaspoon salt
7 tablespoons sweet butter,
softened

Preheat oven to 400°. Butter a large ring mold. Sift ⅔ cup flour into a mixing bowl and make a well in the center. Add 2 yeast cakes, softened in warm water, and stir until well mixed. Gather up the flour and yeast, shape into a flat cake and set it aside.

Sift 2⅓ cups cake flour in the same bowl and make a well in the center. Drop in the eggs, sugar, and salt, and work them into the flour with your fingertips. Put the mixture on a board and beat it vigorously with an up-and-down motion—slapping it on the board as hard as you can for at least 10 minutes. Put the flattened yeast mixture into this dough and continue beating for about 5 minutes, or until the yeast mixture is thoroughly incorporated.

Transfer the dough to the bowl and gradually work in the butter until the dough is smooth and soft.

Pour into a ring mold, cover with a towel, and let rise in a warm place until the dough reaches the top. Bake for 35 to 40 minutes, or until golden. Unmold on a platter.

GLAZE

3 cups water
1 cup sugar
½ cup rum

½ cup warm sieved apricot
preserves
1 cup toasted almond slivers

In a saucepan, combine water with sugar and boil the syrup for 10 minutes. Remove from heat and stir in the rum.

Pour the hot syrup gradually over the entire cake to saturate it completely. Spread top with preserves and sprinkle with almonds.

TOPPING

1 fresh pineapple
2 cups orange juice
1 cup sugar

3 tablespoons cornstarch
1½ cups whipped cream

Peel and cut up pineapple. Cook it with orange juice, sugar, and cornstarch until it is thick and clear. When cooled, add to whipped cream and pass separately when serving the cake.

HOLIDAY FRUIT CAKE

*1 pound dried apricots,
chopped*
1 pound dates, chopped
*1 pound red and green
candied cherries*
*1 pound red and green
candied pineapple*
1 pound golden raisins
*1 pound almonds, blanched,
toasted, and chopped*
*1 pound pecans, broken
into pieces*
4 cups all-purpose flour
1 pound sweet butter
*¾ pound (1½ cups) brown
sugar*

*¾ pound (1½ cups)
granulated sugar*
12 eggs
1 teaspoon ground cloves
2 teaspoons cinnamon
1 teaspoon mace
1½ teaspoons baking soda
1 teaspoon salt
4 tablespoons rum
4 tablespoons curaçao
4 tablespoons brandy
Juice and rind of 2 oranges
Juice and rind of 2 lemons

Preheat oven to 300°. Thoroughly grease four 8" x 5" x 3" loaf pans. Dredge fruits and nuts with 1 cup flour and set aside. Cream butter and sugars. Add eggs one at a time, beating after each addition. Sift remaining flour with spices, baking soda, and salt, and add to creamed mixture alternately with flavorings and juices. Pour into loaf pans. Set the pans in a large pan of water and bake for about 2½ hours.

CHOCOLATE SQUARES

CRUST

½ cup sweet butter, softened   1 cup flour
½ cup brown sugar

Preheat oven to 350°. Mix all ingredients together to form a dough. Press into an 8″ x 8″ pan to form bottom crust, and cover with the following batter.

BATTER

2 eggs, beaten   1 teaspoon baking powder
½ cup granulated sugar   ½ teaspoon salt
3 tablespoons cocoa   1 teaspoon vanilla
2 tablespoons all-purpose
    flour

Combine all ingredients. Pour over the crust and bake for 35 minutes.

FROSTING

1 cup powdered sugar   4 tablespoons sweet butter
4 tablespoons cocoa   1 teaspoon vanilla
1 egg   Hot black coffee, as necessary
2 tablespoons light corn syrup

Mix all ingredients together. If too thick, add a few drops of hot black coffee. Frost the cake, and when it has cooled, cut it in squares.

GLAZED CHOCOLATE MERINGUE IN PETITS FOURS

CAKE

7 eggs, separated
1 tablespoon water
¼ teaspoon salt

½ cup sugar
⅓ cup all-purpose flour
2 tablespoons cocoa

Preheat oven to 375°. Line a 15″ x 10″ jelly-roll pan with buttered waxed paper. Beat egg whites with water and salt until stiff. Gradually beat in the sugar, 1 tablespoon at a time, until thick. Set aside. Beat the yolks until thick and very carefully fold them into the egg whites. Sift flour with the cocoa and fold into the eggs. Pour batter into pan and bake for about 15 minutes, or until the center feels springy when touched. Let the cake cool in the pan for 10 minutes. Invert on wire rack and carefully peel off the paper. Let cake cool completely while making filling and frosting as follows:

FILLING

1 tablespoon gelatin
¼ cup cold water
2½ cups heavy cream
¾ cup powdered sugar

3 squares semisweet chocolate,
  melted
1 teaspoon vanilla
½ cup thick apricot jam

Sprinkle gelatin over cold water in a small bowl to soften. Set the gelatin in a pan of hot water until dissolved. Cool slightly.

Beat the cream until it begins to thicken and pour in the gelatin in a steady stream. Add powdered sugar, chocolate, and vanilla, and beat until stiff.

Cut the cake lengthwise. Cover one half with jam, spread the chocolate filling evenly over the jam, and chill. Meanwhile make the glaze:

GLAZE

2 squares semisweet chocolate   *¼ cup hot water or hot coffee*
½ cup powdered sugar   *1 teaspoon butter*

Melt chocolate in the top of double boiler, set over hot water. Stir in powdered sugar and water (or coffee). Add butter and cook, stirring for about 10 minutes, or until thick enough to spread.

Spread the untouched half of the cake with this glaze and let stand at room temperature for about 1 hour, or until glaze is set.

Just before serving, cut the glazed cake into 14 squares and arrange on top of the chilled cake. With a sharp knife dipped into hot water, cut the squares all the way through.

ORANGE LEBKUCHEN

CAKE

2 eggs
½ cup sugar
2¼ cups all-purpose flour
½ teaspoon baking powder
½ teaspoon cinnamon
½ teaspoon nutmeg

¼ teaspoon cloves
1 cup ground blanched almonds
1 cup honey
½ cup orange juice
1 tablespoon grated orange rind

Preheat oven to 400°. Grease and flour a 15″ x 10″ pan. Beat the eggs in a bowl until light. Gradually beat in the sugar and continue beating until pale in color. Mix together dry ingredients and almonds. Add to beaten eggs alternately with honey and orange juice and rind. Turn into prepared pan. Bake for 15 to 20 minutes. Cool and remove from pan. Glaze the cake as follows:

ORANGE GLAZE

2 tablespoons sweet butter,
*   softened*
1 cup powdered sugar

1 teaspoon grated orange rind
2 tablespoons orange juice

Blend together and beat until smooth.

Spread over top and sides of cake. When glaze is set, cut the cake into squares or finger-length servings.

FRUIT TART
(FRESH STRAWBERRY, RED RASPBERRY,
PEACH OR CHERRY)

CRUST

2 cups graham cracker crumbs ½ cup brown sugar

2 teaspoons cinnamon ½ cup melted sweet butter

Preheat oven to 375°. Thoroughly grease a 9″ spring-form pan. Mix all ingredients and sprinkle on the bottom and sides of the pan. Bake for 12 to 15 minutes. Cool and fill with the following:

FILLING

2 cans sweetened 2 cups whipped cream
condensed milk 1 quart fresh fruit, in
⅔ cup lemon juice bite-size pieces

Beat milk with lemon juice until thick. Fold in 1 cup whipped cream and fruit.

Fill the baked crust and refrigerate for several hours. When tart is thoroughly chilled remove from pan. Put the remaining whipped cream in a pastry tube and decorate the entire top of the tart.

BLUEBERRY-CHEESE TORTE

2 cups graham cracker crumbs

2 teaspoons cinnamon

1½ cups sugar

⅔ cup melted sweet butter

1½ pounds cream cheese

4 eggs

3 teaspoons lemon juice

3 teaspoons fresh lemon rind, grated

1 quart blueberries

¼ cup water

2 teaspoons cornstarch (mixed with 2 tablespoons of the water)

Preheat oven to 350°. Thoroughly grease a 9″ spring-form pan. Mix crumbs with cinnamon, ½ cup sugar, and butter. Press crumbs over bottom and sides of pan.

Beat cheese, adding remaining sugar, eggs, 2 teaspoons lemon juice and rind. Pour mixture into pan. Bake for 35 minutes.

Cool and chill and remove from pan. Combine berries, water, cornstarch, and remaining lemon juice and rind. Simmer until glazy and spread over the cake.

LEMON TORTE

CAKE

1½ cups all-purpose flour

1 cup finely ground toasted blanched almonds

1 cup powdered sugar

½ teaspoon vanilla

¼ teaspoon salt

1 cup sweet butter

In a large bowl combine flour, almonds, powdered sugar, vanilla, salt, butter. Cut ingredients together as you would for making pie crust. When mixture forms a dough, knead it lightly for a few seconds with the heel of the hand to distribute the butter evenly and form a ball. Dust lightly with flour. Wrap in waxed paper and chill for 2 hours.

Preheat oven to 375°. Flour the *backs* of two 9″ layer-cake pans before each baking.

Divide the dough into 5 parts. Roll each part out on a board covered with waxed paper. Bake each part on *back* of pan for about 12 minutes. Don't let the cake brown—it should be just golden. (You can keep the unbaked parts in the refrigerator while baking the first layers.) With a broad spatula, remove the baked layers to a wire rack and let cool.

LEMON GLAZE

1 cup sugar
¾ cup water
2 pounds apples, peeled,
  cored, and chopped

¼ cup lemon juice

In a large saucepan bring sugar and water to a boil. Add apples and lemon juice. Cook the mixture, stirring until thick. Let cool.

Spread on four layers and sandwich them together. Top with remaining layer.

ICING

½ cup powdered sugar
2 tablespoons hot lemon juice

2 tablespoons hot water

In a small mixing bowl, combine powdered sugar, lemon juice and water. Mix until smooth.

Spread immediately on the cake and let stand until set.

LOW-CALORIE FROSTY LEMON TORTE

This recipe is as low-calorie as this book gets.

CRUST

1 cup cookie crumbs	*2 tablespoons sweet butter*

Thoroughly grease the sides and bottom of a 9″ pie pan. Combine ingredients and press into pan.

FILLING

2 eggs, separated	*⅓ cup fresh lemon juice*
⅔ cup sugar	*⅔ cup nonfat milk*
1 tablespoon grated lemon rind	*⅔ cup water*
	½ teaspoon salt

In the bowl of an electric beater, combine the yolks and ½ cup sugar. Beat until thick and lemon-colored. Blend in the lemon rind, lemon juice, and salt.

In another bowl combine egg whites, nonfat milk, water, and remaining sugar. Beat at highest speed until stiff, then fold in the yolk mixture.

Fill the pie crust and sprinkle remaining crumbs over top. Cover and freeze until firm, about 6 hours or overnight.

WALNUT LAYER TORTE

9 eggs, separated
1½ cups powdered sugar
1 teaspoon orange flavoring
Grated rind of 1 orange
1 pound ground walnuts

½ cup fine cake or bread crumbs
1 teaspoon cinnamon
2 teaspoons baking powder
¼ teaspoon salt
1 cup chopped walnuts (optional)

Preheat oven to 375°. Thoroughly grease and flour three 9″ layer-cake pans. Beat egg whites until peaks form. Very gradually add ¾ cup sugar, 1 table-spoon at a time, continuing to beat until all sugar has been used and the mixture is thick. Set aside.

Beat yolks until thick, adding balance of sugar and continuing to beat until thick. Add orange flavoring and rind. Mix nuts with crumbs, cinnamon, baking powder, and salt. Carefully add to yolk mixture and stir until well blended. Fold half of egg white mixture into yolk mixture and add this to the remaining egg whites, carefully folding so you don't break down the air beaten into the whites. Pour mixture into pans. Bake for about 35 minutes, or until the center feels firm. Remove and let cool. Remove from pans, fill with Apricot Purée (page 125) and frost with either rum- or coffee-flavored Chocolate Frosting (page 156).

If you like, sprinkle an additional cup of chopped walnuts around the edges on top and on sides of cake.

DOBOSH TORTE

CAKE

9 large eggs, separated
½ teaspoon salt
1 teaspoon cream of tartar
1½ cups granulated sugar
Grated orange rind

1 teaspoon orange liqueur
1 cup potato flour (sometimes
   called potato starch)
1 tablespoon powdered sugar

Preheat oven to 400°. Thoroughly grease and flour an 11″ x 17″ jelly-roll pan. In a large bowl beat the egg whites until peaks form. Add salt and cream of tartar and continue beating until stiff. Gradually add 1 cup sugar, 1 tablespoon at a time, and continue beating until thick. Set aside.

Beat egg yolks until thick. Add remaining sugar, grated rind, liqueur and potato flour, and continue to beat until thick. Gradually fold the beaten egg whites into the yolk mixture. Pour into pan and bake for 10 minutes. Reduce heat to 350° and bake 10 minutes longer. Remove from oven. When cooled, turn out on waxed paper sprinkled with powdered sugar.

CHOCOLATE FROSTING

1 can sweetened condensed
   milk
⅓ cup fresh lemon juice
6 ounces semisweet chocolate,
   melted

1 teaspoon vanilla
1 teaspoon orange liqueur
1 cup blanched almond slivers,
   toasted

Beat together all ingredients until thick.

Cut the cake crosswise into five portions. Stack sandwich style with frosting in between and on top and sides of cake. Sprinkle with almonds on top and sides.

APRICOT FRUIT TORTE

CAKE

1 cup plus 3 tablespoons
  sifted all-purpose flour
2 tablespoons sugar
½ teaspoon salt
Grated rind of 1 orange
  and 1 lemon

⅔ cup sweet butter
1 tablespoon vinegar
2 tablespoons sour cream
1 No. 2½ can pitted apricot
  halves (reserve juice)

Preheat oven to 400°. Thoroughly grease a 9″ spring-form pan. Into a bowl sift the flour, sugar, and salt. Add rinds. Cut the butter into the dry ingredients, add vinegar and sour cream. If dough is too sticky add a little more flour. Cover and place in refrigerator for 30 minutes.

Roll dough on a floured board to fit the pan. Bake for 30 minutes. Remove from oven and cover with pitted apricot halves.

GLAZE

1 cup apricot juice (reserved
  from can of apricots)
Juice of 1 lemon

1 tablespoon cornstarch
½ cup sugar

Mix all ingredients in saucepan and cook until thick.

Pour over apricot halves and return cake to oven for 20 minutes. Remove from oven and cover with the following:

MERINGUE TOP

3 egg whites

3 tablespoons sugar

4 tablespoons blanched almond slivers

Lower oven to 300°. Beat egg whites until thick. Add sugar, continuing to beat until thick. Spread over the apricot-covered cake. Sprinkle with almond slivers and return to oven for about 15 minutes.

DATE TORTE

CAKE

6 egg whites

½ teaspoon salt

1 cup sugar

3 cups finely chopped walnuts

10 ounces diced dates

1 tablespoon grated orange rind

1 tablespoon orange liqueur

Preheat oven to 375°. Grease a deep 9″ square pan. Beat egg whites with salt until peaks form. Add sugar, 1 tablespoon at a time, continuing to beat until stiff. Combine nuts and dates and very carefully fold into the meringue along with the rind and liqueur. Pour into pan and bake for about 35 minutes. Cool and remove from pan.

FROSTING

1 pint whipped cream
½ cup powdered sugar
1 tablespoon cocoa

2 tablespoons orange liqueur
Candied orange rind, diced

To the whipped cream, add sugar mixed with cocoa and liqueur. Mix until frosting has the consistency for spreading.

Frost cake and sprinkle with orange rind.

PASSOVER ORANGE MERINGUE TORTE

CAKE

1¼ cups egg whites (from
about 10 eggs)
2 cups sugar

1 teaspoon lemon juice
½ teaspoon salt

Preheat oven to 250°. Grease and flour *backs* of two 9″ layer-cake pans. Beat egg whites very gradually until stiff. Add sugar, 1 tablespoon at a time, while continuing to beat. Add lemon juice and salt. With a spatula, spread *backs* of pans, being careful not to spread too close to the rim of the pan, because in baking the meringue spreads a little. Bake for about 1½ hours. Allow meringue layers to cool thoroughly before removing from pans.

FILLING

4 egg yolks	*Grated rind of 1 orange*
½ cup sugar	*2 cups whipping cream*
3 tablespoons orange juice	

Put egg yolks, sugar, orange juice, and rind in top of double boiler and beat over boiling water until thick. Cool. Whip cream and fold 1 cup cream into yolk mixture.

Spread the filling between the meringue layers and garnish with remaining whipped cream.

SUGGESTION: If you wish, grate a little orange rind over the top of the cake or chop some candied orange peel and sprinkle on top.

SACHER TORTE

CAKE

10 eggs, separated	*2 cups ground pecans*
1 cup sugar	*12 ounces semisweet chocolate*
2 tablespoons cake or bread	*2 tablespoons strong*
crumbs	*brewed coffee*

Preheat oven to 350°. Lightly grease and flour three 9″ layer-cake pans. Beat egg yolks with ½ cup sugar until thick and lemon-colored. Add crumbs and nuts. Melt chocolate in hot coffee. Cool, then add to yolk mixture.

Beat egg whites until stiff, very gradually beat in the remaining sugar, then fold into the yolk mixture. Pour into pans and bake for about 35 minutes. Cool on wire rack.

CHOCOLATE FROSTING

4 squares unsweetened chocolate	2 yolks, beaten
½ cup strong brewed coffee	½ cup sweet butter, softened
1 cup sugar	½ cup currant or raspberry jelly

Combine chocolate and coffee in saucepan. Heat until chocolate is dissolved and add sugar. Cook until smooth and thickened, stirring frequently. Remove from heat, beat in yolks and butter, and cool.

Cover two cake layers with a thin coating of jelly and frosting and stack them. Put the third layer on top and cover with the remaining frosting.

PECAN TORTE

PASTRY

2 cups all-purpose flour	1 yeast cake or 1 package dry yeast, dissolved in ¼ cup sweet cream
1 teaspoon sugar	
1 teaspoon salt	
½ pound sweet butter	

Mix flour, sugar, and salt together. Cut butter into dry ingredients as for pie crust. Sprinkle on the yeast and cream and cut in with a knife until the dough forms a ball. Refrigerate while making the filling.

FILLING

6 eggs, separated

½ teaspoon salt

1 cup sugar

2 cups finely ground pecans

Grated rind of 1 orange and 1 lemon

2 teaspoons brandy

Preheat oven to 350°. Lightly flour a 9″ x 12″ pan. Beat egg whites until stiff. Very gradually add ½ cup sugar and continue beating until stiff. Beat yolks until thick and lemon-colored, add salt and remaining sugar, and mix. Fold the yolk mixture into the egg whites, and then fold in the nuts, rind, and brandy.

Remove the dough from the refrigerator. Divide in half. Roll out one portion and cover bottom of pan. Spread it with the filling. Roll out the other portion of dough and place it over the filling. Bake for about 35 minutes. Remove from oven and cool.

ICING

4 tablespoons lemonade, or
    as needed

1 cup powdered sugar

¼ cup chopped nuts

Slowly add lemonade to sugar until it has the consistency for spreading.

Ice the cake and sprinkle with nuts. (Around Christmas, add a few red and green candied cherries.)

CARROT TORTE

I think you will enjoy this cake very much. It remains moist for a long time.

CAKE

12 eggs, separated
1 teaspoon cream of tartar
1 cup sugar
1 tablespoon orange liqueur
Juice and rind of 1 orange

6 tablespoons grated raw carrots
6 tablespoons coarsely grated apple
6 tablespoons grated almonds
1 teaspoon baking powder
½ cup potato starch

Preheat oven to 400°. Lightly flour three 9″ cake pans. Beat egg whites until stiff. Add cream of tartar, gradually add ½ cup sugar, and beat until stiff. Beat yolks until thick, add liqueur, orange juice and rind, grated carrot, apple, almonds, and remaining sugar. Mix baking powder and potato starch and gradually add to yolk mixture. Fold in the egg whites. Pour into pans and bake for 10 minutes. Reduce heat to 350° and bake until done, about 35 minutes. When cool, remove from pans.

FROSTING

¾ pound sweet butter
1 pound powdered sugar
5 eggs
Juice and rind of 2 oranges

2 tablespoons orange liqueur
Dash of salt
Grated pistachio nuts

Cream the butter. Gradually add powdered sugar and beat until smooth. Add eggs, one at a time, beating constantly. Add orange juice and rind, liqueur, and salt. Beat until thick enough to spread. If too thin, add more sugar; if too thick, add more orange juice.

When cake has cooled, fill and frost, and sprinkle with grated pistachio nuts.

NOTE: Pistachio nuts are expensive, so you can substitute colored coconut.

Take ½ cup of coconut meat and chop finely. Put in a glass jar and very cautiously add ½ drop of green vegetable coloring. If you like a deeper shade use a tiny bit more coloring. Shake well and use in place of pistachio nuts.

WALNUT TORTE

CAKE

3 cups sifted all-purpose flour	1 cup sweet butter
¾ cup sugar	1 egg
½ teaspoon salt	

Preheat oven to 350°. Lightly flour the *backs* of two or three 9" layer-cake pans before *each* baking. Combine the dry ingredients in a large bowl. Rub cold butter into this mixture with your fingertips. Break the egg onto the mixture and cut it in. Form the dough into a ball.

Divide ball of dough into 6 equal parts. Roll each part into a 9" circle and bake on inverted pans for 10 to 12 minutes, or until the edges are golden brown. Let layers cool and remove them from the pans with a broad spatula.

FILLING

2 cups ground walnuts
1½ cups powdered sugar
1 teaspoon brandy
2 cups sour cream

1 teaspoon vanilla
Strained apricot preserves
Powdered sugar

Combine walnuts, sugar, brandy, sour cream, and vanilla, and stir until smooth.

Spread the filling over each cake layer except the layer to go on top, and press them together gently. Spread the top of the cake with a thin coating of apricot preserves and sprinkle with powdered sugar. Cut into thin wedges to serve.

CHESTNUT TORTE

CAKE

10 egg whites
1 teaspoon cream of tartar
¾ cup sugar

¼ cup cake flour
½ teaspoon salt
½ cup ground pecans

Preheat oven to 375°. Line a 12″ x 17″ pan with buttered waxed paper. Beat egg whites until frothy. Add the cream of tartar and continue beating until stiff. Add the sugar, 1 tablespoon at a time, beating until the mixture is stiff. Fold in the flour mixed with salt and the ground nuts. Pour into pan and bake for 15 minutes. Let cool for 10 minutes and invert onto a wire rack to cool completely.

CHOCOLATE CHESTNUT CREAM

½ pound plus 2 tablespoons
   sweet butter
1 cup powdered sugar
1 egg
3 squares semisweet
   chocolate, melted

1 pound canned chestnut purée
1 teaspoon vanilla
5 tablespoons rum
Chocolate stars (optional)

In the bowl of an electric mixer combine all ingredients except the chocolate stars. Beat at medium speed until smooth. Chill the cream until it is thick enough to spread.

Carefully peel the paper off and cut the cake lengthwise in 3 parts. Spread two-thirds of the Chestnut Cream over two of the strips. Put one strip on top of the other and top them with the unfrosted strip. Smooth remaining cream over top and sides of cake. Decorate the top with shaved chocolate or the little chocolate stars that you can purchase in the candy department of the supermarket.

FILBERT TORTE

CAKE

8 egg whites
1 teaspoon cream of tartar
1⅓ cups sugar
12 egg yolks

2 cups ground toasted filberts
1 teaspoon instant coffee
3 tablespoons ground or grated
   sweet chocolate

Preheat oven to 350°. Thoroughly grease and flour two 9″ layer-cake pans. Beat egg whites until stiff, adding cream of tartar and ⅓ cup sugar, a little at a time. Set aside.

Beat yolks until very thick, adding the remaining sugar. When mixture is very thick, add filberts, coffee, and chocolate. Fold in the egg whites. Pour into pans and bake for about 45 minutes, or until the center feels springy when touched. Let cool for 10 minutes and invert onto a wire rack to cool completely.

FILBERT FILLING

2 egg whites
⅓ cup sugar
3 tablespoons ground sweet
   chocolate

1 tablespoon finely chopped
   filberts

Beat egg whites until stiff, adding sugar very gradually. Fold in the rest of the ingredients.

Spread the filling between cake layers.

MARASCHINO ICING

2 cups powdered sugar
1 tablespoon sweet butter
3 tablespoons maraschino
   juice

1 tablespoon cream
Maraschino cherries with stems

Blend all ingredients and beat until smooth. If too thick add a little more juice; if too thin add more sugar.

Frost the top and sides of the cake and decorate with maraschino cherries.

HAZELNUT TORTE

CAKE

12 eggs, separated
½ teaspoon salt
1 teaspoon orange liqueur
1 tablespoon orange brandy
2 cups granulated sugar

4 cups ground toasted hazelnuts
½ cup cake or graham cracker
    crumbs
2 teaspoons baking powder
Grated rind of 1 large orange

Preheat oven to 400°. Thoroughly grease and flour three 9″ layer-cake pans. Separate eggs into two bowls. Beat egg whites with salt until peaks form. Very gradually, add 1 cup sugar, 1 tablespoon at a time, beating constantly until thick. Set aside.

Beat yolks until thick and add liqueur, brandy, and remaining sugar. Continue beating. Add nuts mixed with crumbs, baking powder, and orange rind. Put half of egg white mixture into the yolk mixture and cut and fold it in. Fold in the rest of the egg whites until the mixture shows no traces of white.

Pour into pans. Bake for 10 minutes, then reduce the heat to 350° and bake for about 35 minutes longer, or until cake springs back when touched in the center. Remove from oven. Let cool in pans for 10 minutes. Remove from pans and cool thoroughly.

ICING

1 cup shortening	6 whole eggs
½ cup sweet butter, softened	2 teaspoons vanilla
3 cups powdered sugar	4 teaspoons black coffee
1 cup cocoa	2 teaspoons brandy (optional)
¼ teaspoon salt	½ cup red raspberry jam

Cream shortening and butter until fluffy. Gradually add powdered sugar, cocoa, salt, and eggs (one at a time), beating constantly. Add vanilla, black coffee, and brandy until frosting has the consistency for spreading.

Put one layer on a serving plate, spread with the jam and icing. Cover with second layer. Spread again with jam and icing and cover with third layer. Frost the top and sides with the icing. Put remainder of icing in pastry bag with a star tube and make a design around the top edge of cake or shave some chocolate curls from a bar of sweet chocolate and sprinkle the top.

COOKIES

SWEDISH SPRITZ COOKIES

1 cup sweet butter
¾ cup sugar
3 egg yolks
2½ cups all-purpose flour

½ teaspoon baking powder
¼ teaspoon salt
¼ teaspoon almond extract
1 teaspoon vanilla

Preheat oven to 350°. Thoroughly grease baking sheets. Beat the butter until creamy. Gradually add sugar, beating until fluffy. Add yolks, one at a time, beating until smooth. Sift flour with baking powder and salt, and gradually add to butter mixture. Mix until well blended. Add almond extract and vanilla. Place in cookie press and push out dough in small rings onto baking sheets. Bake for 12 minutes.

SOUR CREAM CRESCENTS

1 cup sweet butter, softened
½ cup sugar
1 egg, separated
1 teaspoon grated lemon rind
1 cup finely ground almonds
   or pecans

1 cup sour cream
3 cups all-purpose flour
½ teaspoon cinnamon
1 teaspoon baking soda
1 cup sliced almonds

Cream butter. Add sugar, egg yolk, lemon rind, ground nuts, sour cream, and flour mixed with cinnamon and baking soda. Mix well. Put dough in refrigerator overnight. In the morning, preheat oven to 325° and thoroughly grease and flour cookie sheets.

Shape pieces of dough into 2" crescents. Brush with egg white and sprinkle with or roll in sliced almonds. Bake on cookie sheet for 12 minutes or until lightly browned.

SOUR CREAM COOKIES WITH COCONUT FROSTING

COOKIES

½ cup sweet butter
¾ cup brown sugar
1 egg plus 1 yolk
1½ cups plus 2 tablespoons
   all-purpose flour
1½ teaspoons baking powder

½ teaspoon baking soda
½ teaspoon salt
½ cup sour cream
½ teaspoon vanilla
½ cup chopped pecans

Preheat oven to 375°. Thoroughly grease cookie sheet. In a bowl, cream butter and sugar together. Beat in the whole egg and the yolk. Add flour, baking powder, baking soda, and salt. Combine ingredients well. Add sour cream, vanilla, and pecans. Drop the batter by teaspoonfuls onto a greased cookie sheet and bake for 12 minutes, or until bottoms are golden. Let cool.

FROSTING

1¼ cups powdered sugar
2 tablespoons sweet butter,
  softened

2 tablespoons milk
½ teaspoon vanilla
Shredded coconut

In a bowl, combine sugar and butter, and beat in the milk and vanilla.
  Spread the mixture on the cookies and sprinkle with shredded coconut.

REFRIGERATOR BUTTERSCOTCH COOKIES

1½ cups sweet butter
1 cup granulated sugar
1 cup light brown sugar
2 eggs
1 teaspoon lemon juice
1 teaspoon vanilla

2 tablespoons vinegar
3 cups all-purpose flour
½ teaspoon salt
2 cups chopped toasted blanched
  almonds

Cream butter. Add sugars and eggs, one at a time, beating until well combined. Mix in the lemon juice, vanilla, vinegar, flour, salt, and nuts. Form into long rolls 1" in diameter and refrigerate overnight.

In the morning, preheat oven to 375°. Grease cookie sheets.

Cut dough into slices ¼" thick and bake for about 10 minutes. Lift from cookie sheet carefully. When cooled, store in covered tins.

CHOCOLATE ORANGE DROPS

½ cup sweet butter
3 ounces cream cheese
½ cup powdered sugar
1 egg
1 tablespoon grated orange rind

1 teaspoon vanilla
1 cup sifted all-purpose flour
½ teaspoon salt
6 ounces semisweet chocolate
pieces

Preheat oven to 350°. Thoroughly grease cookie sheets. Butter and cheese should be at room temperature; cream together until light and fluffy. Gradually add sugar and egg, continuing to beat until smooth. Blend in the orange rind and vanilla. Add flour and salt. Fold in the chocolate pieces and drop by teaspoonfuls on cookie sheet. Bake for 10 minutes.

ALMOND GINGER SNAPS

1 cup sweet butter, softened
1 cup sugar
½ cup molasses
1 tablespoon ground ginger
2 teaspoons cinnamon

2 teaspoons ground cloves
1 teaspoon baking soda
1 cup sliced blanched almonds
½ teaspoon salt
3½ cups all-purpose flour

Work butter until creamy. Add sugar, molasses, spices, baking soda, almonds, salt, and flour. Turn onto floured board and knead until smooth. Shape into 2″ thick slightly flattened rolls. Wrap each in waxed paper and chill thoroughly.

Preheat oven to 325°. Grease a cookie sheet.

Cut chilled dough crosswise with a sharp knife into thin slices. Place on baking sheet and bake for 8 to 10 minutes.

TOASTED ALMOND ICEBOX COOKIES

1 pound sweet butter
1 cup granulated sugar
1 cup brown sugar
3 eggs, beaten
1 pound roasted blanched
  almonds

5 cups all-purpose flour
1 tablespoon cinnamon
2 teaspoons baking soda
½ teaspoon salt
1 teaspoon vanilla

Cream butter and the two sugars. Add eggs, nuts, and flour mixed with cinnamon, baking soda, salt, and vanilla. Roll into rolls 2″ thick and 12″ long. Place in refrigerator overnight.

In the morning, preheat oven to 350°. Grease cookie sheets.

Take one roll at a time and cut into slices, about ¼″ thick, and place them on cookie sheets. Bake for about 10 minutes or until lightly browned.

POLISH ALMOND SLICE

COOKIE BASE

1¾ cups sweet butter
1¾ cups sugar
8 hard-cooked yolks, mashed

1 teaspoon vanilla
4 cups sifted all-purpose flour
½ teaspoon salt

Preheat oven to 350°. Grease an 11″ x 16″ jelly-roll pan. Cream butter with sugar. Add yolks and vanilla. Gently stir in the flour and salt. Press dough into pan. Bake about 1 hour.

BUTTER CRUNCH TOPPING

2 cups granulated sugar
2 teaspoons lemon juice
½ cup heavy cream

1 cup sweet butter
3 cups toasted, slivered, blanched
  almonds

Put sugar and lemon juice in a heavy saucepan. Stir in the cream, until the sugar is completely dissolved. Let mixture boil until a little dropped in cold water forms a firm ball. Remove from heat. Add butter and stir in the nuts.

Pour over the baked cookie and return to oven until topping bubbles. Remove from oven, and when cooled, cut into 2″ x 1″ strips.

ALMOND TUILES

4 egg whites
Pinch of salt
⅔ cup sugar
4 tablespoons all-purpose flour

6 tablespoons sweet butter,
  melted and cooled*
½ teaspoon almond extract
1 teaspoon vanilla
1 cup chopped blanched almonds

Preheat oven to 325°. Butter a baking sheet. Beat egg whites with salt until frothy. Add sugar, 1 tablespoon at a time, beating constantly until mixture is stiff. Sift flour over the mixture, folding it in thoroughly but lightly. Add butter mixed with almond extract and vanilla, and add almonds. Fold in thoroughly.

Drop batter by teaspoonfuls in mounds 3" apart on baking sheet. Flatten each mound into a flat 2½" circle. Bake in center of oven for 10 minutes. Using a spatula, remove, one at a time, and curve each piece by pressing it around a rolling pin. Let cool on a wire rack.

* Be sure to use only the top and leave the milky residue in pan.

ALMOND CARAMEL SQUARES

CRUST

1 Short Crust Pastry recipe (page 160).

Make crust and line two 13" x 9" pans. Chill for 1 hour. Preheat oven to 375° and bake for 14 minutes. Let cool.

CARAMEL AND ALMOND TOPPING

1 cup heavy cream   *1 cup sweet butter*
1 cup honey   *4 cups sliced blanched almonds*
3 cups sugar

In a heavy saucepan, combine cream, honey, sugar, and butter. Bring to a boil over moderately low heat, stirring and making sure the sugar is dissolved before the mixture starts to boil. Boil until candy thermometer registers 225°. Add almonds and boil until thermometer registers 240°.

Fill the baked crust with the topping mixture and bake in 375° oven for 20 to 25 minutes, or until the filling is caramel-colored. Let cool and cut in small squares and chill for about 24 hours. These are also attractive placed in individual candy cups.

COCONUT AND WALNUT COOKIES

1 cup sweet butter
1 cup brown sugar
3 eggs
2 cups all-purpose flour
½ teaspoon salt
1 teaspoon baking powder

3 cups crushed corn flakes
1 cup walnuts
½ cup coconut
1 cup sweetened condensed milk
2 teaspoons vanilla

Preheat oven to 375°. Cream butter and sugar until fluffy. Add eggs, one at a time, beating after each addition. Gradually add the flour sifted with salt and baking powder. Add corn flakes, nuts, coconut, milk, and vanilla. Pour into a greased jelly-roll pan or drop by teaspoonfuls onto a greased baking sheet and bake for about 15 minutes. If baked in a pan, cut into bars when ready to serve.

MELT-AWAY FILBERT COOKIES

Portland, Oregon, where I live, is filbert country. We're proud to use these nuts in our baking.

1 8-ounce package cream
 cheese
1 cup sweet butter
2 cups sifted all-purpose flour
¼ cup melted sweet butter
¾ cup light brown sugar

1 tablespoon cinnamon
¾ cup finely chopped filberts,
 toasted in the oven and skins
 removed
1 egg yolk
1 tablespoon water

In a large bowl, blend cheese with butter and flour until dough forms a ball. Chill for about 1 hour.

Preheat oven to 400°. Grease cookie sheets.

Divide dough in fourths. On a floured board, roll out each fourth into a ⅛"-thick 9" circle. Brush each circle with melted butter and sprinkle with about 3 tablespoons brown sugar. Sprinkle with cinnamon and nuts and cut each circle into about 8 wedge-shaped pieces. Roll each from the wide edge to the point and place on a cookie sheet. Brush tops with yolk mixed lightly with water.

Bake in lower middle part of oven for about 18 minutes. Remove and place on racks to cool.

FILBERT SQUARES

Whenever you use filberts, the flavor is improved if the nuts are first roasted and the skins rubbed off. All the skins won't come off, but don't worry about it.

1 cup sweet butter, softened
1 cup plus 3 tablespoons sugar
1 egg, separated
2 cups all-purpose flour

¼ teaspoon ground cardamom
1 cup chopped filberts
1 teaspoon cinnamon

Preheat oven to 300°. Grease a 15" x 10" x 1" baking pan. Cream butter and 1 cup sugar. Beat in egg yolk. Sift flour with cardamom and blend into creamed mixture. Spread in the pan, and press with your hand until smooth. Beat egg white until foamy and brush over top of dough. Sprinkle with filberts to which remaining sugar and cinnamon have been added. Press nuts into dough and bake for 1 hour. Cut into 1½" squares while hot.

DATE FILBERT COOKIES

COOKIES

1 cup sweet butter	*1 teaspoon baking soda*
1½ cups brown sugar	*1 teaspoon cream of tartar*
2 eggs	*½ teaspoon salt*
3½ cups all-purpose flour	*1 teaspoon vanilla*

Preheat oven to 375°. Cream butter and sugar thoroughly. Add eggs, one at a time, and beat until light and fluffy. Beat in the sifted dry ingredients and vanilla. Chill dough several hours.

Roll out to ⅛" thickness a quarter of the dough at a time on a well-floured surface. Cut with a small round fluted cutter.

FILLING

¾ cup finely chopped filberts	*2 tablespoons grated orange rind*
2 cups pitted dates	*and juice*
½ cup sugar	*Dash of salt*
½ cup water	

Preheat oven to 350°. Toast filberts in oven for 5 to 8 minutes. Combine dates, sugar, water, orange juice, rind, and salt. Cook, stirring until thickened, about 5 minutes. Let cool.

Spread 1 teaspoon filling on each round and top with another round, pressing the edges with the tines of a fork. Place on an ungreased sheet and bake for 10 to 12 minutes.

JOE E. BROWNS

Joe E. Brown the comedian was originally from Toledo, Ohio, where we first started our business. I concocted this cookie and named it "Joe E. Brown" because he came into the shop often and this was one of his favorites.

1 pound butter
1 pound light brown sugar
11 eggs
1 pound chopped pecans

½ cup all-purpose flour
½ teaspoon salt
1 teaspoon vanilla

Preheat oven to 350°. Grease cookie sheets. Cream butter, add sugar, and beat until light and fluffy. Add eggs, one at a time, beating after each addition. Stir in the pecans, flour, salt, and vanilla. Drop the batter by teaspoonfuls on cookie sheets. Put only about 4 cookies on a sheet at a time, and be sure to beat the batter each time you take some. Bake about 12 to 15 minutes or until light brown. Remove each cookie with a metal spatula and roll up like a cigar. If cookies get too brittle to roll, return to oven for a few minutes and again start rolling. The process is a little slow at first, but as you continue to work, you'll become more proficient and it will go much faster. When cooled, be sure to keep these cookies in a covered can.

CRISP PECAN LATKE

If you want to, when you take these pecan latkes from the oven, wait a minute and lay each over the back of a cup until cooled. Remove and you can use them as containers for ice cream or other desserts.

1 cup firmly packed brown
sugar
1 cup melted sweet butter
1 cup light corn syrup

2 cups all-purpose flour
2 cups finely chopped pecans
3 teaspoons vanilla

Preheat oven to 350°. Thoroughly grease cookie sheets. In a 2-quart saucepan, combine sugar, butter, and corn syrup. Cook over high heat, stirring constantly, until mixture comes to a boil. Remove from heat and stir in flour and nuts until blended. Mix in the vanilla.

Drop batter by level teaspoonfuls about 3" apart onto cookie sheets, and bake for about 8 minutes, or until cookies are a rich golden brown. Cool about 1 minute, remove from pan, and cool on racks. These keep best in a covered can.

MOCHA PECAN COOKIES

1½ *cups all-purpose flour*   2 *teaspoons instant coffee*
½ *cup sugar*   1 *cup sweet butter*
¼ *teaspoon salt*   2½ *cups chopped pecans*

Preheat oven to 300°. Grease a cookie sheet. Sift flour, sugar, salt, and instant coffee. Cut in the butter until bits are the size of peas. Press dough together. Pinch off small pieces, shape into balls about the size of large marbles and roll in chopped nuts. Place the dough balls 2″ apart on cookie sheets and flatten with a glass dipped in granulated sugar. Bake for about 20 minutes or until edges are lightly browned. Cool thoroughly before storing.

DATE AND NUT RUM BALLS

These make a very attractive platter of petits fours.

CAKE

8 *eggs*   ½ *teaspoon salt*
2 *cups sugar*   1 *teaspoon baking powder*
1 *pound pecan pieces*   1 *teaspoon baking soda*
1 *pound chopped dates*   ¾ *cup **rum***
4 *cups all-purpose flour*

104

Preheat oven to 350°. Beat eggs until thick. Gradually beat in the sugar, then add the nuts, dates, and the flour mixed with salt, baking powder, and baking soda. Blend thoroughly. Pour into an ungreased jelly-roll pan and bake for about 35 minutes. Remove from oven and sprinkle with rum. When dough has cooled enough to handle with a teaspoon, scoop out a small portion and roll each into a ball.

ICING

3 cups powdered sugar
½ cup orange juice
2 tablespoons rum
1 cup chopped toasted almonds

1 cup shredded coconut
1 cup chopped pecans
1 cup chocolate shot

Mix the sugar, juice, and rum together.

Dip each ball into this mixture, then into the chopped nuts, coconut or chocolate shot—you can leave some of the balls plain or you can let your imagination run wild. When the topping has set, place balls in colored paper candy cups.

ICING FOR FLOWERS

On the plain balls, use your pastry bag fitted with a star tube. Make little flowers in different colors.

2 cups powdered sugar   *½ cup cream*

Blend together. If icing is too thin, use more sugar. Icing should be thick enough to hold its shape. Add a drop of food coloring for varied effects.

SESAME SEED GLAZED COOKIES

FILLING

2 cups ground pecans
½ cup ground toasted
    almonds
1 cup sugar

1 egg
1½ teaspoons cinnamon
½ teaspoon ground cloves

Mix together all ingredients. Set aside while mixing the dough.

COOKIES

1 cup melted sweet butter
½ cup white wine
½ cup water
½ cup sugar
¼ teaspoon salt

4½ cups all-purpose flour
1 teaspoon baking powder
½ cup sesame seeds
1 cup honey
½ cup water

Preheat oven to 400°. In a large bowl, combine butter, wine, water, sugar, and salt. Gradually add flour sifted with baking powder. Stir until the flour is completely absorbed and the dough is moist but not sticky.

Break off pieces of dough the size of a small walnut, and with the fingers, press each piece into a flat 1½″ circle. Put ½ teaspoon nut filling in the center of each circle and fold the edges of the dough over the filling, pressing the edges together. Hold each half circle between thumb and forefinger and shape into a crescent. Arrange the crescents about ½″ apart on an ungreased baking sheet and bake for 20 to 25 minutes, or until golden brown.

In a skillet, heat sesame seeds until golden. In a 2-quart saucepan, combine honey with water. Bring syrup to a boil and simmer gently for 15 minutes.

Drop the baked cookies into the boiling honey syrup and simmer for about 2 minutes, or until they are well glazed. Remove the cookies to a platter and sprinkle them at once with the toasted sesame seeds.

SLICE-AND-SERVE COOKIES

COOKIE BASE

1 cup dates
2/3 cup plus 1 tablespoon
   sifted all-purpose flour
3 eggs
3/4 cup sugar
1/2 teaspoon baking powder

1/2 teaspoon salt
1/2 cup pecan pieces
1 teaspoon vanilla
20 maraschino cherries, drained
Powdered sugar

Preheat oven to 325°. Line a 15" x 10" jelly-roll pan with greased waxed paper. Sprinkle dates with 1 tablespoon flour. Beat eggs until thick, add sugar, beating constantly. Fold in the dry ingredients, pecan pieces, vanilla, and dates. Spread batter in pan. Arrange 10 cherries across each end about 1/2" from edge of pan. Bake for 25 to 35 minutes.

Remove from oven and immediately turn out cake on waxed paper sprinkled with powdered sugar. Remove paper, trim edges of cake, and cut crosswise into two rectangles. Beginning with the cherry end, roll each rectangle tightly. Wrap in waxed paper and cool before frosting.

FROSTING

1½ *cups powdered sugar*
2 *tablespoons light cream*

½ *teaspoon vanilla*
Chopped pecans

Mix together all ingredients except pecans until smooth. Spread cooled roll thinly with frosting and roll in pecans. Chill to serve in ½″ slices.

ROCKS À LA TAVEL

6½ *cups all-purpose flour*
2 *cups golden raisins*
2 *cups pecan pieces*
1 *pound sweet butter*
3 *cups brown sugar*
6 *eggs*

2 *teaspoons cinnamon*
1 *teaspoon ground cloves*
1 *teaspoon salt*
2 *teaspoons baking soda dissolved*
   in 3 tablespoons hot water
2 *teaspoons vanilla*

Preheat oven to 350°. Thoroughly grease cookie sheets. Mix flour with raisins and nuts, and set aside. Cream butter. Add sugar gradually, then eggs. Stir in remaining ingredients and then blend in the floured raisins and nuts. Drop by teaspoonfuls onto cookie sheets and bake for 10 to 12 minutes.

CHOCOLATE FUDGE SQUARES

COOKIE

1 cup sweet butter
6 1-ounce squares unsweetened
chocolate
2 cups sugar

6 eggs, beaten until light
1 cup all-purpose flour
2 teaspoons vanilla
2 cups chopped pecans

Preheat oven to 350°. Grease an 11″ x 17″ x 1½″ pan. Melt butter and chocolate in a saucepan. Add sugar to eggs and beat until thick. Add flour and vanilla, stirring well. Blend in the chocolate-butter mixture and beat well. Add vanilla and pecans and pour into pan. Bake for 25 minutes. Remove from oven and let cool.

CHOCOLATE FROSTING

4 unsweetened chocolate
squares, melted
1 cup powdered sugar
1 tablespoon corn syrup

2 tablespoons sweet butter
4 tablespoons strong coffee
1 teaspoon vanilla

Beat together all ingredients.
Spread over the chocolate cake. When cooled, cut into 1″ squares.

FUDGE BROWNIES

2 tablespoons cocoa

1 cup brown sugar

1 egg, beaten

¼ cup melted sweet butter

1 teaspoon vanilla

1 cup chopped nuts

½ cup sifted flour

Preheat oven to 325°. Thoroughly grease an 8″ x 8″ x 2″ pan. Mix all ingredients together, beating until smooth. Pour into pan and bake for about 20 minutes. Remove from oven and cut into squares.

FUDGE NUT SQUARES

These are very rich and delicious.

COOKIE BASE

1 cup sweet butter

2 cups brown sugar

2 eggs

3 teaspoons vanilla

2½ cups all-purpose flour

1 teaspoon baking soda

1 teaspoon salt

3 cups rolled oats

1 cup chopped pecans

Preheat oven to 350°. Grease a 10″ x 16″ pan. Cream together the butter and brown sugar. Add eggs and vanilla. Beat well. Sift together the flour, baking soda, and salt. Add to butter-and-sugar mixture. Add rolled oats. Press two-thirds of this cookie mixture into a pan.

FILLING

1 12-ounce package chocolate chips

1 15-ounce can sweetened condensed milk

3 tablespoons butter

¾ cup chopped pecans

1 teaspoon vanilla

Melt chocolate bits, canned milk, and butter in a double boiler over hot water. Add pecans and vanilla.

Pour filling onto cookie mixture. Sprinkle remaining cookie mixture over the filling and bake for 20 to 25 minutes. Do not overbake. Cut in small squares and place in paper candy cups.

NEAPOLITAN COOKIES

These sound complicated and they do take time, but they are worth the trouble.

DARK DOUGH

6 ounces semisweet
   chocolate pieces
1 cup sweet butter
1½ cups brown sugar
½ teaspoon cinnamon
½ teaspoon ground cloves

2 eggs
3 cups sifted all-purpose flour
1 teaspoon salt
1 teaspoon baking soda
1 cup finely chopped nuts

Melt chocolate pieces in a double boiler over hot but not boiling water. Remove from heat.

Cream together butter, sugar, and spices until light and fluffy. Beat in the eggs, one at a time, beating well after each addition. Blend in the melted chocolate. Sift together flour, salt, and baking soda. Stir into the creamed mixture. Add nuts and set aside while mixing the light dough.

LIGHT DOUGH

¾ cup granulated sugar
½ cup sweet butter
1 egg
2 tablespoons water
1 teaspoon vanilla
½ teaspoon almond extract

2 cups all-purpose flour
½ teaspoon salt
¼ teaspoon baking soda
¾ cup finely chopped raisins
12 finely chopped candied
   cherries

Cream sugar and butter together. Beat in egg, water, vanilla, and almond extract.

Sift together the flour, salt, and baking soda. Stir into the butter-sugar-egg mixture. Add raisins and cherries. Blend well.

Pack half of the dark dough into a 9" x 5" x 3" bread pan lined with waxed paper. Add all of the light dough, packing it evenly over the dark dough. Place remaining dark dough on top. Cover the top with waxed paper and place in refrigerator overnight.

In the morning, preheat oven to 400°. Grease a cookie sheet.

Remove dough from pan, remove the waxed paper, and cut the dough lengthwise in thirds. Keep one third out. Put the rest back in refrigerator (if dough gets warm, it's difficult to cut).

Slice the dough crosswise in ¼" slices. Place on cookie sheet and bake for 8 to 10 minutes. Repeat the process with the refrigerated dough. Be sure to remove cookies from pans as soon as baked. When cooled, put in cans for best keeping.

HALF-AND-HALF COOKIES

½ cup sweet butter, softened
¾ cup brown sugar
¼ cup granulated sugar
2 eggs, separated
1 teaspoon vanilla
1 cup all-purpose flour

¼ teaspoon salt
⅛ teaspoon baking soda
½ teaspoon baking powder
1 6-ounce package semisweet
  chocolate bits

Preheat oven to 350°. Butter a 12″ x 8″ x 2″ pan. Mix butter with ¼ cup each of brown and granulated sugar until fluffy. Add egg yolks and vanilla. Sift flour, salt, baking soda, and baking powder and add to batter. Place in pan and top with chocolate bits.

Beat egg whites until stiff, adding remaining brown sugar. Spread over topping and bake for 30 minutes. Cut into squares while warm.

AUSTRIAN PEACH COOKIE

These cookies decorate a cookie tray beautifully. A real conversation piece, they take time and patience, but the results are very satisfying and exciting.

¾ cup sweet butter	*¼ cup chocolate pieces, melted*
½ cup milk	*and cooled*
1 cup sugar	*⅓ cup ground pecans*
2 eggs	*2 teaspoons rum or sherry*
1 teaspoon baking powder	*¼ cup water*
·3¾ cups all-purpose flour	*⅓ cup red sugar**
1 teaspoon vanilla	*⅔ cup yellow-orange sugar**
⅔ cup apricot jam	*Green stems***

* You can purchase the colored sugars or you can put a little sugar in two small pans and sprinkle a drop of red coloring in one and orange coloring in the other. Stir until well mixed.
** You can purchase green stems.

Preheat oven to 325°. Put butter, milk, sugar, eggs, baking powder, and 2 cups flour in the bowl of an electric mixer. Blend 1 minute on low speed, scraping the bowl constantly, then beat 1 minute on medium speed while continuing to scrape the bowl. Stir in the remaining flour and vanilla. Dough will be smooth and soft.

Shape dough into smooth ¾″ balls (each ball will make half a peach). Place balls 1″ apart on ungreased baking sheet. Bake in center of oven until cookies are brown on the bottom, about 15 to 20 minutes. Cool on wire racks.

Place the tip of a small knife in the center of the flat side of each cookie and carefully rotate to make a hollow. Reserve crumbs that fall off. Mix 1½ cups of the crumbs with jam, chocolate, nuts, and rum. Fill the hollowed cookies with the crumb mixture.

Set 2 filled cookies, flat sides together, to make a peach. Press together gently. Brush each peach lightly with water. Immediately roll one side of the peach in red sugar for blush. Sprinkle yellow-orange sugar on the peach to cover completely. Insert a green stem at the top. Set aside to dry.

BRANDY DATE BONBONS

18 pitted dates
½ cup chopped, toasted
  blanched almonds
½ cup chopped pecans
2 cups all-purpose flour
1 cup sweet butter, softened

½ cup brown sugar
2 tablespoons brandy
½ teaspoon salt
2 eggs, separated
Glazed cherries

Chop the dates and mix with nuts. Dust with flour. Cream butter. Add sugar, brandy, salt, and egg yolks. Mix in the nuts and dates, and stir until well blended. Chill for 1 hour for easier handling.

Preheat oven to 350°. Grease cookie sheets.

Shape dough into ¾″ balls. Brush with slightly beaten egg whites and top with glazed cherries. Bake for 10 to 12 minutes. Cool and place in individual paper candy cups.

DIAGONALS

1 cup sweet butter, softened   2½ cups all-purpose flour
½ cup sugar   ½ teaspoon salt
1 egg yolk   Currant jelly

Preheat oven to 350°. Cream butter and sugar until fluffy. Add egg yolks, flour, and salt. Mix thoroughly and cool.

Roll out one-third of the dough into 2 strips about 2½″ wide. Place on greased cookie sheet. Force remaining dough through pastry tube to make 3 rows on each strip. Bake until golden. When cold, force currant jelly through pastry bag between rows. Cut into 1″ diagonals.

BRANDY RINGS

1⅓ cups sweet butter,
  softened
¾ cup powdered sugar

3½ cups all-purpose flour
3 tablespoons brandy
½ teaspoon salt

Preheat oven to 350°. Grease cookie sheets. Mix together all ingredients and work until smooth. Turn onto a floured board and roll into thin lengths.

    Take 2 lengths at a time and twist together like twine. Cut into 4″ to 5″ pieces and shape into rings. Place on cookie sheet and bake for about 10 minutes or until golden.

CHOCOLATE LEAVES

COOKIES

4½ tablespoons sweet
  butter, softened
4½ tablespoons sugar
6 tablespoons finely ground
  blanched almonds

1 egg, beaten
¾ cup all-purpose flour
1 teaspoon rum or brandy

117

Preheat oven to 300°. In a mixing bowl, beat butter with a wire whisk until it is light and creamy. Gradually add sugar and continue beating the mixture until it is white and fluffy. Stir in almonds and egg. Blend in flour and flavoring.

Lay a greased leaf-shaped metal stencil (which can be purchased in the household section of department stores) flat on a well-buttered and floured baking sheet. With a spatula, spread 2 tablespoons of the dough over the stencil. Press down on the dough, scrape off excess dough, and lift the stencil straight up into the air leaving the leaf-shaped cookie on the sheet. Clean the stencil and continue making the leaves until all the dough is used. Bake for 10 to 15 minutes, or until edges are delicately golden. Remove from baking sheet while still warm and cool on a cake rack.

ICING

4 ounces dark sweet chocolate

In the top of a double boiler over hot water, melt chocolate and stir briefly with a spatula.

Ice the cookie leaves. With a toothpick, draw lines resembling the veining on a leaf. Let set and store in covered cans. These will keep for weeks.

MACAROONS

COOKIE BASE

1 1/4 cups all-purpose flour
1/4 cup sugar
1/2 teaspoon salt

1/2 cup sweet butter
1 tablespoon cream
1 teaspoon vanilla

Grease cookie sheets. Combine flour, sugar, and salt. Cut in the butter. Add cream and vanilla. Mix dough until it forms a ball and roll thin on a lightly floured board. Cut out dough with 2½″ cutter. Place on cookie sheet and spread with the following:

TOPPING

1/2 cup ground toasted
  almonds
1/2 cup granulated sugar
2 egg whites

1/8 teaspoon salt
1 teaspoon vanilla
Currant jelly

Preheat oven to 350°. Combine nuts, sugar, egg whites, and salt in a saucepan. Stir over very low heat for about 10 minutes, or until mixture leaves a clear path for a second when spatula is drawn across pan. Do not allow mixture to boil. Remove from heat and blend in vanilla.

Place a teaspoonful of the topping on each cookie and bake for about 12 to 15 minutes. Remove from heat and put ½ teaspoon currant jelly in the center of each cookie.

ALMOND MACAROONS

1½ pounds canned almond
   paste
1 cup powdered sugar
1 cup granulated sugar
½ cup ground, toasted
   blanched almonds
½ teaspoon salt
1 teaspoon cinnamon

Grated rind of 1 orange and
   1 lemon
Juice of 1 lemon
2 teaspoons brandy
½ cup egg whites
Glazed red cherries or
   blanched almond halves

Thoroughly grease and flour a baking sheet. Cream the almond paste. Gradually add sugar, ground almonds, salt, cinnamon, orange and lemon rind and juice, brandy, and egg whites. Beat until mixture is thick. Put it into a star-pointed pastry bag and squeeze bits of it out onto a baking sheet. Top each piece with a glazed red cherry or blanched half almond. Leave covered overnight.

In the morning, preheat oven to 325° and bake for about 20 minutes or until lightly browned. Macaroons should be brown outside but soft and chewy inside.

FRENCH MACAROON-TYPE COOKIES

2 egg whites

1 cup sugar

1 teaspoon vinegar

1 cup finely chopped pecans

1 cup finely chopped walnuts

Preheat oven to 325°. Grease a baking sheet. Beat egg whites until stiff with an electric mixer. Very gradually add the sugar, 1 tablespoon at a time, continuing to beat until thick. Add vinegar and fold in the nuts. Put mixture in top of double boiler and heat over boiling water, stirring for 8 minutes, or until slightly thickened. Cool and shape with a teaspoon or roll between your hands to form into sticks about 2½" long (for easier handling, rinse hands in cold water). Bake on cookie sheet for 5 to 7 minutes.

SWEDISH MACAROONS

You can decorate these cookies with red or green cherries or with whole blanched almonds if you like.

1⅓ cups finely ground
    blanched almonds

1½ cups powdered sugar

Grated lemon rind

Dash of salt

2 egg whites

Preheat oven to 300°. Grease cookie sheets. Mix together dry ingredients, then add egg whites and mix. Force dough through star-tipped pastry bag onto cookie sheet. Bake for about 30 minutes. These should be light golden brown but soft inside. Remove from cookie sheet while warm.

FILBERT ALMOND KISSES

COOKIES

4 egg whites
1 cup sugar
2 cups finely ground shelled
   filberts

1 cup ground almonds
1 teaspoon vanilla
Dash of salt

Grease cookie sheets. Beat egg whites until stiff. Gradually add sugar, 1 tablespoon at a time, and beat until very stiff. Fold in the nuts carefully. Add vanilla and salt and chill for several hours. Drop by teaspoonfuls 1" apart onto cookie sheet.

TOPPING

1 egg white
1 cup sifted powdered sugar
½ teaspoon vanilla

Dash of salt
Filberts

Preheat oven to 275°. Beat egg white until stiff, and gradually add sugar, vanilla, and salt.

Spread the mixture on top of the cookies and press a filbert into the center of each. Bake for 15 to 20 minutes, or until lightly browned.

ALMOND RUSKS

2 eggs
¾ cup sugar
⅔ cup chopped blanched
   almonds

1½ cups all-purpose flour
1 teaspoon baking powder
¼ teaspoon salt

Preheat oven to 350°. Thoroughly grease a baking sheet. Beat eggs and sugar until thick. Add almonds and flour mixed with baking powder and salt. Stir until well blended. Pour mixture onto baking sheet in two 1½″ rows. Bake for 10 minutes. Remove from oven and cut into ½″ slices; separate slices. Reduce heat to 250° and bake for 8 more minutes. Turn off heat and leave in oven to dry, about 20 minutes.

ALMOND WAFERS

⅔ cup blanched almonds
½ cup sugar
½ cup sweet butter

1 tablespoon all-purpose flour
2 tablespoons milk

Preheat oven to 350°. Thoroughly grease a cookie sheet. Grind almonds. Mix with all other ingredients in skillet, stirring until butter melts. Drop by teaspoonfuls about 4" apart on cookie sheet. Bake for 8 to 10 minutes, or until light brown. Allow to cool slightly and then press over a wooden spoon handle to shape into a curled wafer or you can roll up each cookie like a cigar.

APRICOT DAINTIES

¾ cup chopped apricots

1 cup orange juice

2 cups sugar

10 tablespoons sweet butter

1 teaspoon vanilla

Grated rind of 1 orange

2 eggs

2 cups all-purpose flour

1 teaspoon baking powder

½ teaspoon salt

1 cup sour cream

1 teaspoon baking soda

Powdered sugar

Preheat oven to 350°. Grease a 9" pan. Combine apricots with orange juice and ½ cup sugar. Boil and simmer for 20 minutes. Beat until smooth and add 2 tablespoons butter. Beat together the remaining butter and sugar. Add vanilla and orange rind. Beat in eggs, one at a time. Sift flour, baking powder, and salt. Add to creamed mixture alternately with the sour cream mixed with baking soda. Beat after each addition. Pour the batter in the pan and spoon apricot sauce evenly over it. Bake for about 1 hour and 10 minutes. Remove from oven, turn upside down (the bottom becomes the top), and sprinkle with powdered sugar. Cut as desired.

APRICOT TURNOVERS

DOUGH

2 cups sweet butter
4 cups all-purpose flour
Grated rind of 2 lemons

½ teaspoon salt
1 pint sour cream

Cream butter and flour. Add lemon rind, salt, and sour cream. At first the dough seems very moist, but as you keep beating with a wooden spoon it becomes more solid. Roll into individual balls the size of walnuts and refrigerate overnight.

In the morning, preheat oven to 400°. Grease a baking sheet. While oven is heating, make the filling:

APRICOT PURÉE

8 ounces dried apricots
2 tablespoons orange juice
1 cup sugar

1 tablespoon brandy
Grated rind of 1 orange

Put apricots and orange juice in blender and purée. Mix with remaining ingredients.

Roll out each ball of dough and fill with the purée. (You don't have to use all the dough at once. Leave the dough you don't use in the refrigerator or freezer.) Place turnovers on baking sheet and bake for about 30 minutes.

MOCHA ACORNS

1 cup sweet butter
¾ cup brown sugar
2½ cups all-purpose flour
1 teaspoon cocoa
1 teaspoon instant coffee

1 teaspoon vanilla
¼ teaspoon salt
6 ounces semisweet chocolate
    pieces, melted
1 cup chopped pecan pieces

Preheat oven to 325°. Grease cookie sheets. Cream butter and brown sugar. Add the sifted flour, cocoa, instant coffee, vanilla, and salt. Mix well. Roll into 4 long rolls about 1″ in diameter. Cut into ¾″ sections and roll each into a ball. With fingertips, press each ball slightly onto the cookie sheet to make a flat base and pinch the top to make a point (balls shouldn't be more than ¾″ in diameter). Bake for 10 to 12 minutes. While warm, dip the wide end of the balls into chocolate and roll in the pecans. Place in paper candy cups.

WALNUT BRANDY CONES

½ cup sweet butter
⅓ cup light corn syrup
½ cup granulated sugar
2 tablespoons brandy

½ cup all-purpose flour
¼ teaspoon salt
½ cup finely chopped walnuts

Preheat oven to 350°. Thoroughly grease cookie sheets. Combine butter, corn syrup, and sugar in a 2-quart saucepan. Heat slowly until butter is melted. Cool to lukewarm. Add brandy, flour, and salt and beat until smooth. Stir in the walnuts.

Bake 4 cookies at a time, dropping teaspoonfuls about 6″ apart on a cookie sheet. Bake for about 6 to 8 minutes, or until brown and bubbly. Allow to cool about 1 minute, and with a spatula, remove from cookie sheet and roll into a cone. If cookies get too crisp to roll, return to the oven for a moment before rolling.

These are very fragile and delicious and will remain crisp if stored in a tin cookie can.

FRENCH LACE CONES

This cookie is very attractive and a little different.

1 cup sifted all-purpose flour   *½ cup light corn syrup*
1 cup finely chopped pecans*   *⅔ cup light brown sugar*
½ cup butter

Preheat oven to 325°. Grease cookie sheets. Combine flour and nuts. Melt butter in a saucepan. Add corn syrup and sugar and bring to the boiling point. Remove from heat and blend in the flour and nuts. Drop teaspoonfuls of batter about 3″ apart onto cookie sheets. Bake for 8 to 10 minutes. Cool 1 minute. Remove carefully with a large spatula and roll each cookie at once to form a cone.

* Do not grind—this will make you lose all the oil.

CARAMEL FILLING

1 tablespoon unflavored
    gelatin
¼ cup cold heavy cream
⅓ cup sweet butter
1 cup dark brown sugar

1 egg, well beaten
¼ cup heavy cream, whipped
1 teaspoon vanilla
Chopped pecans or grated
    sweet chocolate

Dissolve gelatin in cold heavy cream. Set over hot water to dissolve thoroughly. Let cool.

Meanwhile, cream butter with sugar. Add egg and dissolved gelatin, then fold in the whipped cream and vanilla. Set in refrigerator until filling has thickened.

Stuff each cookie cone with the filling and sprinkle with chopped nuts or grated chocolate. Or you can fill the cones with ice cream. Either way, keep the cones in the freezer.

BRANDY NUT STICKS
(HUNGARIAN)

These cookies take patience but the result is well worth the trouble.

DOUGH

2 cups sweet butter, softened
1 cup powdered sugar
3 egg yolks

2 tablespoons brandy
4 cups all-purpose flour
½ teaspoon salt

Cream butter with sugar. Add yolks, one at a time, beating well after each addition. Add brandy and then the flour and salt. Mix until smooth. Chill for easier handling.

FILLING

1 pound toasted pecans or
* almonds*
2 cups sugar

3 tablespoons brandy
4 tablespoons sweet butter
Powdered sugar

Preheat oven to 375°. Grease cookie sheets. Grind nuts in blender. Remove and put in the sugar, brandy, and butter. Add the nuts. If too thick, add more brandy, but be careful not to thin too much.

Take a small portion of the chilled dough and form into balls the size of walnuts. Roll out each ball on a lightly floured board until paper-thin. (Remove dough from refrigerator a little at a time for easier handling.) Take the filling 1 teaspoon at a time and roll between your hands until pencil-slim and as long as the flattened pieces of dough. Place the filling at one end of each piece of dough and fold the top and sides to enclose the filling. Roll up each piece tightly to resemble a thin pencil about 4″ long. Place on cookie sheets and bake for about 15 minutes (be careful not to overbake). When cooled, sprinkle with powdered sugar. When thoroughly cooled, place in airtight cans.

PECAN LOGS

½ pound sweet butter
½ cup powdered sugar
2 cups chopped pecans

½ teaspoon salt
1 cup all-purpose flour
1 teaspoon vanilla

Preheat oven to 325°. Thoroughly grease a baking sheet. Cream butter. Add sugar, pecans, salt, flour, and vanilla. Taking a teaspoonful at a time, form small balls and roll these between your hands into 2″ logs. Place on baking sheet and bake for about 20 minutes, or until just lightly golden. When cooled, sprinkle with powdered sugar.

LEMON SNOWBALLS

COOKIES

1 cup sweet butter
½ cup powdered sugar
1½ cups all-purpose flour
¾ cup cornstarch

2 teaspoons grated lemon rind
1 cup finely chopped, toasted
    blanched almonds
¼ teaspoon salt

Preheat oven to 350°. Grease cookie sheets. Cream butter with sugar. Add flour sifted with cornstarch and salt. Mix in the lemon rind. Shape into 1″ balls and roll in the chopped nuts, pressing them in. Bake for about 15 minutes. Cool on wire rack.

FROSTING

1 cup powdered sugar

2 tablespoons melted sweet
   butter

1 tablespoon lemon juice

Stir all ingredients together and spread on the cookies.

MOCHA NUT BUTTERBALLS

1 cup sweet butter, softened

½ cup granulated sugar

2 teaspoons vanilla

2 cups finely chopped pecans

2 teaspoons instant coffee

¼ cup cocoa

1 ¾ cups all-purpose flour

½ teaspoon salt

Powdered sugar

Preheat oven to 325°. Thoroughly grease cookie sheets. Cream butter and sugar. Add vanilla, nuts, coffee, cocoa, flour, and salt. Shape into 1″ balls and bake on cookie sheet for 15 minutes. When cooled, roll in powdered sugar.

GERMAN NUT BALLS

These are attractive and freeze well.

1 cup sweet butter
½ cup powdered sugar
2 cups ground almonds
1 vanilla bean, ground
2 cups all-purpose flour

½ teaspoon salt
1 egg, beaten
1 cup chopped pecans
Glazed red cherries, halved

Preheat oven to 350°. Thoroughly grease cookie sheets. Cream butter, adding powdered sugar, almonds, and vanilla bean. Add flour and salt.

Roll teaspoonfuls of dough into 1" balls. Dip in the egg and then in the pecans. Press cherry halves onto the center of each cookie. Place on cookie sheet and bake for about 25 minutes. You can put these in paper candy cups before serving.

CHOCOLATE PECAN BALLS

COOKIES

1¼ cups sweet butter
1 cup powdered sugar
½ cup cocoa

2 cups all-purpose flour
1 teaspoon vanilla
1½ cups chopped pecans

Cream butter and sugar. Add cocoa, flour, vanilla, and pecans, Refrigerate for about 1 hour for easier handling.

Preheat oven to 350°. Grease a baking sheet.

Pinch off pieces of dough the size of marbles. Bake for 30 minutes. Remove from oven and let cool.

FROSTING

2 cups powdered sugar   2 tablespoons sweet butter
¼ cup cocoa   1 teaspoon light corn syrup
4 tablespoons brewed coffee   1 teaspoon vanilla

Beat all ingredients until smooth and frost the pecan balls.

PEPPERMINT CANDY COOKIES

DOUGH

1 cup sweet butter   ½ cup chopped nuts
½ cup powdered sugar   1 teaspoon vanilla
2½ cups all-purpose flour

Cream butter with sugar. Gradually add flour, nuts, and vanilla. Mix thoroughly. Chill.

FILLING

½ cup crushed peppermint   2 tablespoons cream cheese
  candy   1 teaspoon milk
½ cup powdered sugar   1 drop red food coloring

Preheat oven to 350°. Combine candy and sugar. Blend together cream cheese and milk and add to three-quarters of the candy mixture. Add food coloring. Mix well.

Remove dough from refrigerator. Shape into balls. Make a deep hole with your thumb in the center of each ball and fill with about ¼ teaspoon filling. Seal and place on an ungreased baking sheet. Bake for 12 to 15 minutes, or until set but not brown.

FROSTING

1 cup powdered sugar   ¼ teaspoon peppermint flavoring
                                   Crushed peppermint candy (optional)

Mix sugar and flavoring. Sprinkle flavored sugar on cookies while they are still hot. Top with crushed candy if desired.

DATE AND ALMOND DAINTIES

1 pound finely cut dates
½ pound chopped, toasted
   blanched almonds
½ pound sugar
2 egg whites

1 teaspoon vanilla
⅛ teaspoon salt
1 tablespoon rum
Candied cherries, halved

Mix dates, nuts, sugar, egg whites, vanilla, salt, and rum. Place in refrigerator for 1 hour.

Preheat oven to 300°. Butter cookie sheets.

Form into small cones and top each with half a cherry. Place on cookie sheet and bake for 15 minutes.

GLAZE

4 tablespoons light corn syrup   *2 tablespoons brandy*

Boil ingredients together in a saucepan for 5 minutes.

With a pastry brush, spread the glaze on the cookies while still warm.

CHOCOLATE-FROSTED FINGERS

COOKIES

3/4 cup sweet butter, softened
1/3 cup sugar
3/4 cup ground, toasted
    blanched almonds
1 2/3 cups all-purpose flour
1 teaspoon cinnamon

1/4 teaspoon salt
1/4 cup finely chopped, candied
    orange peel
1 teaspoon grated orange rind
1 cup semisweet chocolate,
    melted

Preheat oven to 325°. Thoroughly grease and flour cookie sheets. Cream butter. Add sugar and almonds and beat until light. Combine flour, cinnamon, salt, candied peel, and rind. Add to butter mixture and blend well.

On a lightly floured board, divide dough into 8 equal pieces. Divide each piece in half and roll into 12"-long ropes. Cut in 2" lengths and put on cookie sheets. Bake about 15 minutes, or until lightly browned. Let cool. Spread with melted chocolate, then sprinkle with the following:

MOCK PISTACHIO NUTS

1 cup ground blanched almonds   1 drop green food coloring

Put nuts and food coloring in a covered container. Shake until nuts are a pale green. Use as a garnish.

PECAN COOKIES

1 pound sweet butter
1½ cups sugar
6 eggs, separated
1 teaspoon vanilla

½ teaspoon salt
4 cups all-purpose flour
2 cups chopped pecans
Chocolate pieces

Preheat oven to 375°. Grease cookie sheets. Cream butter. Add sugar and egg yolks, one at a time, beating constantly. Mix in the vanilla, salt, and flour. Beat egg whites slightly. Shape dough into balls the size of walnuts and dip in the egg whites and then in the chopped nuts. Place on greased cookie sheets and bake for about 10 minutes. Remove from oven, and when cooled, put a chocolate piece in the center of each cookie. Put in paper candy cups to serve.

FRUIT CAKE COOKIES

1½ cups golden raisins
¼ cup diced citron
½ pound chopped candied
    cherries
¼ cup rum
½ cup sweet butter, softened
½ cup brown sugar
2 eggs

1½ cups all-purpose flour
½ teaspoon baking soda
2 teaspoons cinnamon
½ teaspoon ground cloves
½ teaspoon nutmeg
⅛ teaspoon salt
½ pound pecan pieces

Put raisins, citron, and cherries in a bowl. Pour on the rum and let stand for 1 hour.

Cream the butter. Add sugar and eggs and beat until fluffy. Sift flour with baking soda, spices, and salt. Add to the butter mixture and blend well. Add nuts and the rum-soaked fruit. Cover and refrigerate overnight.

In the morning, preheat oven to 325°. Grease cookie sheets.

Form batter into balls the size of walnuts. Bake on cookie sheets for 10 to 12 minutes. Cool on racks. Sprinkle with powdered sugar and place in paper candy cups.

APRICOT STRUDEL

DOUGH

1 cup sweet butter	1 teaspoon salt
1 cup sour cream	2 cups all-purpose flour

Mix together all ingredients. Chill overnight. In the morning, roll dough as thin as possible on a floured board (I find it easier to do this on floured waxed paper).

FILLING

1 pound dried apricots	1 cup shredded coconut
½ cup orange juice	½ cup diced maraschino cherries
¼ cup sugar	½ cup chopped nuts

138

Preheat oven to 350°. Soak apricots in orange juice until soft. Do not cook. Drain and put through grinder or blender with sugar. Combine with remaining ingredients.

Spread the filling on the dough, roll it up like a jelly roll, and place in a shallow greased pan. Bake for 45 minutes. When cool, sprinkle with powdered sugar and cut in 1" slices.

CHOCOLATE MERINGUE BARS

1 cup sweet butter	1 teaspoon baking soda
½ cup granulated sugar	1 tablespoon water
1½ cups brown sugar	1 teaspoon vanilla
2 eggs, separated	1 cup chocolate chips
2 cups all-purpose flour	1 cup chopped nuts
½ teaspoon salt	

Preheat oven to 350°. Grease a 10" x 15" jelly-roll pan. Cream butter, granulated sugar, and ½ cup brown sugar. Add egg yolks, one at a time, and beat until light. Sift flour, salt, and baking soda together, add to butter mixture and beat. Add water and vanilla. Pour into pan and sprinkle with chocolate chips. Press chips in gently.

Beat egg whites until stiff and gradually add remaining brown sugar. Spread over cookie mixture and sprinkle with nuts. Bake for 20 minutes.

CHOCOLATE CHIP BARS

1 cup sweet butter
1 cup sugar
2 cups all-purpose flour
1 teaspoon baking powder

½ teaspoon salt
1 cup semisweet chocolate pieces
½ cup chopped pecans
1 teaspoon vanilla

Preheat oven to 350°. Thoroughly grease and flavor a 9″ x 13″ pan. Cream butter with sugar. Sift together dry ingredients and blend in the chocolate pieces and nuts. Add to butter-sugar mixture with the vanilla. Press onto bottom of pan and bake for about 35 minutes. While still warm, cut into bars. You can either leave these plain or spread with topping made from 6 squares semisweet chocolate melted with 4 ounces sweet butter.

CHOCOLATE ALMOND BARS

2 egg whites
1⅓ cups sugar
1 ounce unsweetened
    chocolate, melted

½ teaspoon cinnamon
2¼ cups ground almonds

Preheat oven to 350°. Grease cookie sheets. Beat egg whites until foamy with an electric mixer. Gradually add 1 cup sugar and continue beating until stiff peaks form. Carefully stir in the chocolate, cinnamon, and nuts to make a rather stiff dough.

Sprinkle remaining sugar on a board. Turn dough out and knead 1 minute, or until well mixed. Pat to about 6″ x 4″. Turn dough over again with enough sugar on the board so that it does not stick. Pat dough into 12″ x 8″ rectangle and cut into 2″ x 1″ bars. Place bars on cookie sheets and let stand for 1 hour or until surface is dry.

Bake for about 10 minutes. The bars should be soft in the middle and crusty on the outside.

LEMON TOFFEE BARS

⅓ cup sweet butter, softened
⅔ cup sugar
2 eggs
1 cup all-purpose flour

¼ teaspoon salt
¾ teaspoon baking powder
1 teaspoon grated lemon peel

Preheat oven to 350°. Thoroughly grease a 9″ square pan. Beat together butter and sugar until smooth. Add eggs and continue beating until well blended. Add sifted flour, salt, baking powder, and lemon peel. Spread in pan and bake for 30 minutes. Cool in pan.

ALMOND TOPPING

½ cup toasted almond slivers
3 tablespoons sweet butter
⅓ cup brown sugar

1 tablespoon all-purpose flour
1 tablespoon heavy cream

Combine all ingredients in a saucepan and cook over low heat, stirring until bubbly.

Spread over the toffee bars and place the pan 5″ from the broiler until topping bubbles (be careful that it doesn't burn). Cool and cut into bite-sized squares and place in candy paper cups.

TOFFEE NUT BARS

CRUST

½ cup sweet butter, softened   1 cup sifted all-purpose flour
½ cup brown sugar

Preheat oven to 350°. Mix the butter and sugar thoroughly. Cut in the flour. Press and flatten with the hand to cover the bottom of an ungreased 13″ x 9″ x 2″ pan. Bake for 10 minutes.

TOPPING

2 eggs   ½ teaspoon salt
1 cup brown sugar   1 cup shredded coconut
1 teaspoon vanilla   1 cup chopped, toasted almonds
2 tablespoons all-purpose flour   Powdered sugar
1 teaspoon baking powder

Thoroughly mix all ingredients except powdered sugar.

Spread over the baked crust and bake for 25 minutes. Cool slightly, then cut into bars and sprinkle with powdered sugar.

CARAMEL ALMOND BARS

CRUST

1¾ cups sweet butter

1¾ cups sugar

8 hard-cooked yolks, mashed

1 teaspoon vanilla

4 cups all-purpose flour

½ teaspoon salt

Preheat oven to 350°. Thoroughly grease and flour an 11″ x 16″ jelly-roll pan. Cream the butter. Add sugar, mashed egg yolks, and vanilla. Carefully stir in flour mixed with salt. Spread the dough in the pan and press it down. Bake for 50 to 60 minutes.

CARAMEL CRUNCH TOPPING

1 tablespoon lemon juice

2 cups granulated sugar

½ cup heavy cream

1 cup sweet butter

2½ cups toasted blanched almond slivers

2 teaspoons vanilla

In a heavy 2-quart saucepan, combine lemon juice, sugar, and cream. Stir over medium heat until sugar is dissolved. Add butter. Wash down the sides of the pan with a brush dipped in hot water, then continue to cook until the mixture starts to color or a few drops in cold water form a soft ball. Remove from heat and add toasted nuts and vanilla.

Pour over baked crust and return to oven until topping starts to bubble. Remove from oven and let cool. Cut into 1″ x 2″ bars.

SEVEN-LAYER BARS

These are called seven-layer bars because the ingredients are layered, not mixed.

¼ cup sweet butter
1 cup graham cracker crumbs
1 cup shredded coconut
*1 6-ounce package semisweet
    chocolate pieces*

*1 6-ounce package butterscotch
    pieces*
*1 15-ounce can sweetened condensed
    milk*
1 cup chopped nuts

Preheat oven to 350°. Melt butter in a 13″ x 9″ pan. Sprinkle crumbs evenly over the melted butter and press down. Sprinkle on the coconut, then the chocolate and then the butterscotch pieces. Pour milk evenly over all. Sprinkle on the nuts and press lightly. Bake for 30 minutes. Cool in pan and cut into bars.

APRICOT BARS

1 cup dried apricots
1 cup water
½ cup sweet butter
¼ cup granulated sugar
1⅓ cups all-purpose flour
2 eggs

1 cup light brown sugar
¼ teaspoon salt
½ teaspoon baking powder
½ teaspoon vanilla
½ cup chopped pecans

144

Preheat oven to 350°. Thoroughly grease a 9″ x 9″ x 2″ pan. Rinse apricots. Cover with water and simmer for 10 minutes. Cool and chop coarsely. Combine butter, granulated sugar, and 1 cup flour. Blend together in small bowl until crumbly. Pack in bottom of pan. Bake for 15 minutes.

Meanwhile, beat eggs. Add brown sugar and remaining flour, salt and baking powder. Add vanilla, nuts, and apricots. Blend all together. Spread on baked layer and bake for 30 minutes more. Cut in bars and sprinkle with powdered sugar. These bars freeze well.

COOKIE CRUMB BARS (NO BAKE)

1 cup plus 1 tablespoon
   sweet butter
½ cup sugar
5 tablespoons cocoa
2 teaspoons vanilla
1 egg, slightly beaten
2 cups cookie crumbs or
   graham cracker crumbs

½ cup chopped pecans
1 cup shredded coconut
1½ cups powdered sugar
3 egg yolks
3 squares semisweet chocolate,
   melted

Thoroughly grease a jelly-roll pan. Put ½ cup butter, sugar, cocoa, 1 teaspoon vanilla, and egg in top of double boiler over hot, not boiling, water. Cook until butter melts. Add crumbs, nuts, and coconut. Blend well. Pack tightly into pan and refrigerate for 2 hours until firm.

Combine ½ cup softened butter, powdered sugar, egg yolks, and remaining vanilla. Beat until smooth. Put this on top of first layer. Pack well and refrigerate until firm.

Melt chocolate with 1 tablespoon butter. Spread over first two layers. Refrigerate until ready to serve. Cut into diamond shapes about 20 minutes before serving.

CHOCOLATE LAYER COOKIES

COOKIE LAYER

2 ounces unsweetened
   chocolate
½ cup sweet butter
2 eggs

1 cup sugar
½ cup sliced unblanched almonds
½ cup unsifted all-purpose flour

Preheat oven to 350°. Thoroughly grease a 9″ square pan. Melt chocolate and butter together over hot water. In a bowl, beat together the eggs and sugar until thick. Add nuts, flour, and chocolate mixture and stir until smooth. Pour batter into pan and bake for 25 minutes. Let cool.

MINT CREAM FILLING

1½ cups powdered sugar
3 tablespoons sweet butter,
   softened

2 tablespoons heavy cream
¾ teaspoon peppermint flavoring

Beat together all the ingredients until smooth. If you like, sprinkle a drop of green coloring into this mint cream.

Spread the filling evenly over the cookie layer, cover and chill until firm, about 1 hour.

CHOCOLATE GLAZE

2 ounces sweet chocolate   1 teaspoon vanilla
2 tablespoons butter

Melt together all ingredients over hot water.

Drizzle the glaze over the mint topping. Cover and chill again until firm. Cut the layer into bite-sized squares and place in paper candy cups.

SWEDISH KRUMKAKOR

You can buy a Krumkakor iron or an electric iron in the household section of some large department stores. I found an Italian electric machine similar to a waffle iron and it works beautifully with much less effort.

Making these cookies takes a little practice, so don't get discouraged. The more you make them the easier it will become. You can leave these plain or you can make a soft chocolate frosting and dip in it the ends of each little cake.

1 cup sweet butter   ½ teaspoon salt
⅔ cup sugar   1 teaspoon vanilla
3 eggs   ½ cup milk
1 cup all-purpose flour

Thoroughly grease a Krumkakor iron. Cream butter with sugar. Beat in eggs, one at a time, and add flour, salt, vanilla, and milk. Beat until smooth.

Heat iron on top of stove, first one side and then the other. Put one scant teaspoon of batter on each of the three sections, close and cook over low heat until batter is light brown on one side. Turn over and finish cooking on other side. It takes about 2 minutes on each side. Remove and cut in thirds. Very quickly roll up into little logs. Should the cookie get too crispy, return to heat for another minute.

CHEESE CAKE DIAMONDS

5 tablespoons sweet butter
⅓ cup brown sugar
1 cup all-purpose flour
¼ cup chopped pecans
½ cup granulated sugar
8 ounces cream cheese,
  softened

1 egg
2 tablespoons cream
1 tablespoon lemon juice
Grated rind of 1 lemon
½ teaspoon vanilla

Preheat oven to 350°. Lightly grease an 8″ x 8″ x 2″ baking pan. Cream butter and brown sugar. Add flour and pecans. Mix well. Set aside 1 cup of mixture for topping. Press remainder into bottom of pan. Bake for 12 to 15 minutes.

Blend granulated sugar and cream cheese until smooth. Add egg, cream, lemon juice and rind, and vanilla. Beat well. Spread over baked crust and sprinkle with reserved cup of topping. Return to oven and bake 25 minutes more. Cool, then chill and cut into diamonds to serve.

APRICOT CRESCENTS

I always keep a split vanilla bean in cans containing granulated and powdered sugar. This way your sugars are always flavored. Purchase your vanilla bean at any supermarket in the flavoring department.

FILLING

1 8-ounce package of
dried apricots

½ cup orange juice
½ cup sugar

Soak apricots in orange juice about 1 hour. Then boil apricots and juice with sugar for about 30 minutes. Blend into a purée. If it is too thin, add cookie crumbs until thick enough so it doesn't run.

DOUGH

1 package yeast
½ cup milk, scalded and
cooled to lukewarm
3 cups all-purpose flour
1 tablespoon sugar

½ teaspoon salt
1 egg, slightly beaten
1 teaspoon vanilla
1 cup sweet butter
Powdered sugar

Preheat oven to 350°. Grease a cookie sheet. Dissolve yeast in lukewarm milk. In a large bowl, sift flour, sugar, and salt. Add egg and vanilla and stir. Cut in the butter until the dough resembles coarse crumbs. Add yeast mixture and stir until dough forms a ball.

149

Divide dough into 4 parts. Roll out each part into a 9″ circle on a board sprinkled with powdered sugar. Cut each circle into 10 parts, pie fashion. Fill with apricot filling, and starting at the wide end, roll toward the point. Form into a crescent shape as you place each piece on the pan. Let stand 10 minutes, then bake for 10 to 12 minutes. Remove crescents immediately from pan, and when cooled, sift powdered sugar over them.

CARAQUE COOKIES

COOKIES

1¾ cups sweet butter, softened	¾ cup sugar
½ teaspoon salt	6 large yolks
2 teaspoons vanilla	3¾ cups sifted all-purpose flour

Preheat oven to 350°. Lightly grease cookie sheets. Mix butter with salt and vanilla. Gradually blend in the sugar. Beat in the egg yolks, two at a time, and stir in the flour, mixing well after each addition. Shape the dough into a ball. Place on a pastry board, invert a bowl over the dough and let stand for 1 hour.

Divide the dough into 3 equal parts. Place 1 part at a time on a lightly floured board (keep the remaining dough under the bowl). Roll each part ⅛″ to ¼″ thick. Cut into round cookies with a 1½″ cookie cutter. Place on cookie sheets and bake for 10 to 15 minutes, or until cookies are lightly browned. Cool on a wire rack.

FILLING

1 can sweetened condensed
   milk
1 teaspoon vanilla

1 12-ounce package semisweet
   chocolate bits, melted
1 cup chopped pecans

Beat all together. When cold, spread between cookies sandwich style.

ICING (Optional)

1 cup powdered sugar
1 tablespoon light corn syrup

¼ cup grenadine
2 tablespoons sweet butter

Combine all these ingredients and ice the cookies.

LEMON SQUARES

At Christmas time you can sprinkle these squares with chopped red and green cherries instead of nuts.

COOKIE LAYER

3 eggs, separated
1 cup sifted powdered sugar
½ cup sweet butter
1 cup granulated sugar
1½ cups sifted all-purpose
   flour

½ teaspoon salt
¼ teaspoon baking powder
½ cup chopped pecans
⅓ cup fresh lemon juice
2 tablespoons grated lemon rind

Preheat oven to 375°. Thoroughly grease and flour a 13″ x 9″ x 2″ pan. Beat egg whites until stiff. Very gradually add powdered sugar and beat until the mixture has the consistency of thick meringue. Set aside. Cream the butter. Add granulated sugar and egg yolks, one at a time, beating after each addition. Sift flour with salt and baking powder. Add to butter mixture alternately with the pecans, lemon juice, and rind. Fold in the egg whites.

Pour into pan and bake for 25 to 30 minutes. Frost while warm.

BUTTER FROSTING

2 tablespoons sweet butter   *1 tablespoon cream*
1 cup sifted powdered sugar   *¼ cup pecan pieces*

Beat together all ingredients except pecans until smooth.

Frost the cookie layer and sprinkle with pecans. When thoroughly cooled, cut into 1½″ squares and place in paper candy cups.

TROPIC SURPRISES

2 cups all-purpose flour   *1 to 2 tablespoons milk*
⅓ cup sugar   *1 teaspoon vanilla*
½ teaspoon baking powder   *½ cup pineapple preserves*
¼ teaspoon baking soda   *½ cup semisweet chocolate*
¼ teaspoon salt   *pieces*
½ cup sweet butter   *½ cup chopped pecans*
1 egg   *Powdered sugar*

Preheat oven to 350°. Grease a baking sheet. Sift dry ingredients into a large bowl. Blend in the butter until the mixture resembles coarse crumbs. Add egg, milk, and vanilla and mix well. For easier handling, chill the dough for about 1 hour.

Shape the dough into a ball, cut in two, and put one half back in the refrigerator. Divide dough into 3 equal parts. Roll out one portion on a well-floured surface to a 12" x 4" rectangle. Spread with ¼ cup pineapple preserves. Roll out a second portion, place on top of the first piece and spread with ¼ cup chocolate pieces. Roll the third portion, place on top of the second piece and spread with ¼ cup pecans. Roll from the long side as for jelly roll. Seal edges and ends, and place seam side down on baking sheet. Repeat with remaining dough in refrigerator. Bake for about 15 minutes. When cool, slice into ¾" pieces. Sprinkle with powdered sugar.

CHOCOLATE HI-HATS (SMALL SQUARE CAKES)

CAKE

1½ cups all-purpose flour
1 cup brown sugar
½ cup sweet butter
⅔ cup hot water
½ cup chopped pecans
1 teaspoon salt

1 teaspoon baking soda
1 egg
2 ounces unsweetened chocolate, melted
½ cup maraschino cherries, halved
12 large marshmallows, halved

153

Preheat oven to 350°. Thoroughly grease and flour a 9″ x 13″ pan. Combine in a mixing bowl all the above ingredients except marshmallows and beat at medium speed for a few minutes. Spread in pan and bake for 25 to 30 minutes, or until top springs back when touched lightly. Remove from oven and immediately arrange marshmallow halves cut side down on top of cake. Cut cake into small squares with marshmallows in the center of each.

CHOCOLATE FROSTING

1 ounce unsweetened chocolate	*1 tablespoon milk*
	1 cup powdered sugar
2 tablespoons sweet butter	

Melt together chocolate and butter with milk. Stir in sugar. Add more milk if needed.

Place a spoonful of frosting on top of each marshmallow.

CARAMEL NUT ACORNS

1 cup sweet butter	*⅓ cup chopped pecans*
¾ cup firmly packed brown sugar	*2½ cups sifted all-purpose flour*
	½ teaspoon baking powder
1 teaspoon vanilla	*3 egg yolks*

Preheat oven to 350°. Melt butter in large saucepan. Add brown sugar, vanilla, pecans, dry ingredients, and egg yolks. Mix thoroughly.

Shape into balls. With a teaspoon, flatten one side of each ball by pressing it on an ungreased baking sheet. Pinch the top to a point to resemble an acorn. Bake for 15 to 18 minutes.

CARAMEL COATING

½ pound caramels
¼ cup water

¾ cup finely chopped pecan pieces

Heat caramels and water in top of double boiler until melted.

Dip ends of acorns in this mixture, then into pecan pieces. When thoroughly cooled and set, place cookies in paper candy cups.

CHOCOLATE ALMOND MANDELBROT

COOKIES

3 eggs
¾ cup sugar
1 teaspoon grated orange rind
1 tablespoon orange juice
1 teaspoon almond extract
2¾ cups all-purpose flour

¼ teaspoon salt
2 teaspoons baking powder
6 tablespoons peanut oil
½ cup split blanched almonds
¼ cup cocoa

Preheat oven to 325°. Thoroughly butter a cookie sheet. In a large bowl, beat the eggs with the sugar until thick. Stir in the orange rind and juice and almond extract.

Sift the flour with salt and baking powder. Fold half the flour mixture into the egg mixture with the peanut oil. Add the remaining flour, and with an electric mixer beat the mixture at medium speed for 30 seconds.

Separate one-quarter of the dough, stir into it the almonds and cocoa, and form into a roll about ½" thick and envelop the cocoa roll with it. Cut the roll in half. Put the rolls side by side on a cookie sheet and bake for 30 minutes. Remove from oven and cut horizontally into ½" thick slices while still hot. Put the slices back on a buttered cookie sheet and bake for 5 more minutes.

CHOCOLATE FROSTING

This chocolate frosting is simple and a little different.

8 ounces sweet chocolate	*2 tablespoons powdered sugar*
1 cup milk	*1 tablespoon marshmallow whip*
2 tablespoons sweet butter	*1 teaspoon vanilla or rum or coffee*

In a saucepan, combine chocolate with milk, butter, and sugar. Cook the mixture over moderate heat, stirring constantly until very thick. Remove from heat and stir in the marshmallow whip and flavoring.

Frost the top of the cookie slices.

156

VIENNA SLICES

2 cups all-purpose flour
1/4 teaspoon salt
1 teaspoon baking powder
1 cup sugar
2/3 cup sweet butter

4 eggs, separated
2 tablespoons milk
1 teaspoon lemon extract
1/2 cup apricot jam
1 cup chopped pecans

Preheat oven to 350°. Sift flour, salt, baking powder, and 1/2 cup sugar. Cut in the butter as if for pie crust. Combine slightly beaten yolks, milk, and lemon extract. Add to dry ingredients and mix well. Put the dough in a 9″ x 12″ x 2″ pan and press it onto bottom and sides to about 1/2″ thickness. Spread jam on top. Gradually beat remaining sugar into beaten egg whites until stiff. Spread over jam and sprinkle nuts on top. Bake for 30 minutes. When cool, cut into 2″ slices.

VANILLA HORNS

For the holidays you can ice the horns with white frosting and dip them in red and green sugar instead of using chocolate.

1/2 cup sweet butter
1/3 cup sifted powdered sugar
1 egg yolk
1 teaspoon vanilla

1 cup plus 2 tablespoons sifted
    all-purpose flour
1/4 cup semisweet chocolate
1 teaspoon cream

Preheat oven to 400°. Thoroughly grease cookie sheets. Cream the butter and sugar and add egg yolk and vanilla. Beat well, and add the flour. Chill if desired.

Shape the dough, 1 teaspoon at a time, by rolling between your hands into 3″ strips and taper one end to curve like a horn. Roll in the sugar and place on cookie sheets. Bake for 8 minutes. Remove from cookie sheets and cool.

Melt chocolate with cream over hot water and stir until cool. Dip the larger end of the horns in chocolate. Cool.

LACY FRENCH COOKIES

1 6-ounce package semisweet
   chocolate pieces
¾ cup sweet butter
¾ cup sugar
¼ teaspoon salt

¼ teaspoon ginger
1 cup all-purpose flour
½ cup chopped almonds
½ cup light corn syrup
1 cup whipped cream

Preheat oven to 350°. Thoroughly grease cookie sheets. Combine chocolate, butter, sugar, salt, and ginger in top of double boiler. Melt over hot but not boiling water. Remove from heat. Gradually stir in flour and nuts. Add corn syrup and mix well.

Drop 4 or 5 teaspoonfuls of dough 3″ apart on each cookie sheet and bake for about 8 to 10 minutes. Cool slightly. Remove with a spatula and lay over a wooden spoon handle or use your fingers to form a cone. When ready to serve, fill the cones with whipped cream and garnish with crushed peppermint. (I take an empty egg carton, cover it with foil, and as I fill each cone I stick it in an egg hole and quickly serve.)

NOTE: If you fill these too far in advance the cones are likely to lose their crispness. If you wish to store the cones, you shouldn't, of course, fill them.

CHOCOLATE ALMOND CUPS

CRUST

¾ cup sweet butter
½ cup sugar
2 cups sifted all-purpose flour

¼ teaspoon salt
1 teaspoon vanilla

Preheat oven to 350°. Thoroughly grease bottom and sides of 3 dozen very small tart shells or muffin pans with small cups.

Cream butter and sugar well. Gradually add flour, salt, and vanilla. Press the dough into shells or muffin cups.

BROWNIE-NUT FILLING

¾ cup almonds
1 cup semisweet chocolate
   pieces

¼ teaspoon salt
2 eggs
½ cup sugar

Grind together the almonds, chocolate, and salt. Beat eggs until thick, and add sugar. Combine with nut-chocolate mixture.

Put a rounded teaspoon of the filling in each shell or cup and bake for about 20 minutes.

159

TOPPING (Optional)

1 cup whipped cream   ½ teaspoon vanilla
2 tablespoons powdered sugar

Mix ingredients together, put in a star-tipped pastry bag, and when cookies
and cold, decorate them.

RASPBERRY-FILLED COOKIES

These are very short and very popular.

SHORT CRUST PASTRY

1 pound butter   2 teaspoons vanilla
1 cup sugar   ½ teaspoon salt
4 egg yolks   5⅓ cups all-purpose flour
Grated rind of 2 lemons

In a bowl of an electric mixer, cream together butter and sugar until mixture
is light and fluffy. Add yolks, one at a time, beating well after each addition.
Add lemon rind, vanilla, and salt. Blend in 4 cups of the flour, 1 cup at a
time. Transfer the mixture to a lightly floured board and knead in the
remaining flour. Wrap the dough in waxed paper and chill for one hour.

FILLING AND ICING

Strained red raspberry
  preserves
1 cup powdered sugar

Juice of 2 lemons
Pecan halves

Preheat oven to 375°. Roll the chilled dough ¼" thick and cut with a round 2" cookie cutter. Bake until lightly browned, about 12 minutes. Spread the bottom side of half of the rounds with raspberry preserves and cover with the remaining rounds. Mix sugar and lemon juice together until smooth and ice the cookies. Top each with a pecan half.

FUDGE TARTS

CRUST

1 cup sifted all-purpose flour
¼ teaspoon baking powder
¼ teaspoon salt

⅓ cup sweet butter
3 to 4 tablespoons beaten egg

Sift together the dry ingredients and cut in the butter until the dough is the size of large peas. Sprinkle on the beaten egg, stirring with a knife until the dough forms a ball. Roll out on a floured surface to about ⅛" thickness. Cut in 3" rounds to fit into very small muffin pans.

FILLING

1 cup semisweet chocolate
  pieces
⅓ cup sugar
1 teaspoon vanilla

1 tablespoon milk
1 tablespoon sweet butter
1 egg, beaten
Pecan halves

Preheat oven to 350°. Combine all ingredients, except the egg and pecans, in double boiler and cook over low heat until chocolate is melted and mixture is smooth. Remove from heat and blend in the egg.

Place a scant tablespoon of filling in each pastry shell and top with half a pecan. Bake for 15 to 20 minutes.

PECAN TARTS

3 ounces cream cheese
½ cup sweet butter, softened

1 cup sifted all-purpose flour
⅓ cup chopped pecans

Preheat oven to 350°. Mix cream cheese, butter, and flour. Chill for easier handling. Shape 2 dozen 1″ balls and place in ungreased muffin pans with cups 3″ or 4″ in diameter. Press dough onto bottom and sides of cups and put ⅓ cup pecans on top.

FILLING

¾ cup brown sugar
1 egg
1 teaspoon vanilla

1 tablespoon sweet butter, softened
¼ teaspoon salt
⅓ cup chopped pecans

162

Beat all ingredients together until smooth.

Sprinkle ⅓ cup pecans on top of filling and bake for 25 to 30 minutes or until filling is set and the crust is browned. Loosen the edges slightly with a knife and cool before removing from pans. These can be placed in fluted paper cups.

RUM CHOCOLATE PUFFS

PUFFS

1 cup water	*½ teaspoon salt*
½ cup sweet butter	*1 cup all-purpose flour*
1 teaspoon sugar	*4 large eggs*

Preheat oven to 425°. Thoroughly grease and flour a cookie sheet. In a 2-quart saucepan, combine water with butter, sugar, and salt and bring to a rolling boil. Add the flour all at one time. Cook until mixture is so thick that it leaves the sides of the pan. Remove from heat and add eggs, one at a time, beating hard after each addition.

Drop the dough from a tablespoon into 12 puffs onto the baking sheet and bake for 15 minutes. Reduce heat to 375° and bake 15 to 20 minutes longer. Remove from oven and let cool.

FILLING

2 eggs
3/4 cup sugar
2 cups milk
1/2 cup cocoa

3 tablespoons cornstarch
1/2 cup whipped cream
1 teaspoon rum
Powdered sugar

In top of double boiler, beat eggs with sugar. Add milk mixed with cocoa and cornstarch and cook until mixture is thick. Cool completely and fold in the whipped cream and rum.

Cut a slit in the bottom of each puff and put the filling into a pastry bag fitted with a plain tube. Insert the tube into the slit of each puff, and press out the filling. Sprinkle the top of each puff with a little powdered sugar.

CHOCOLATE PECAN MERINGUES

4 egg whites
1 teaspoon vinegar
1/4 teaspoon salt
1 cup sugar

2 cups semisweet chocolate
  bits, melted
1 teaspoon vanilla
1 1/2 cups chopped pecans

Preheat oven to 350°. Thoroughly grease cookie sheets. In a large bowl, beat egg whites until foamy. Add vinegar and salt. Continue beating until the whites are stiff, then very gradually add the sugar and keep beating until very stiff. Fold in the melted chocolate, vanilla, and pecans. Drop by teaspoonfuls onto cookie sheet and bake for about 10 minutes.

TEA TOPICS

COOKIES

1½ cups sifted all-purpose
  flour
½ cup sifted powdered sugar
½ teaspoon salt

⅔ cup sweet butter
2 tablespoons cold orange juice
½ teaspoon vanilla

Place dry ingredients in a bowl and cut in the butter until the dough is the size of peas. Cut in the juice and vanilla. Place in refrigerator for 30 minutes for easier handling.

Preheat oven to 350°.

Remove dough from refrigerator. Roll into ⅛″ thickness and cut into 3″ rounds. Fit these rounds into small muffin pans and bake for 12 to 15 minutes.

CARAMEL FILLING

½ pound (28) caramels
2 tablespoons milk

2 tablespoons peanut butter

In top of double boiler, combine caramels and milk. Cook over boiling water until caramels are melted. Stir in the peanut butter. Cool slightly. Fill each cookie round with 1 teaspoon of the filling. Place cookies in paper candy cups.

BUTTER FINGERS

1 cup sweet butter, softened
1 cup sugar
2 eggs, one separated
3 cups all-purpose flour
1 teaspoon salt

1 teaspoon rum or almond
  flavoring
1 cup chopped, toasted blanched
  almonds
1 teaspoon cinnamon

Preheat oven to 375°. Thoroughly grease cookie sheets. Cream butter with ½ cup sugar. Add egg and egg yolk and beat until fluffy. Sift flour and salt together and add to butter mixture. Add flavoring. Mix the chopped nuts, the remaining sugar, and cinnamon. Set aside.

To shape cookies, measure ¼ cup dough at a time and roll on a slightly floured board to a cylinder about 18" long and ½" in diameter. Brush each cylinder with egg white and roll in the nut mixture. Place on cookie sheets and bake for 15 minutes. As soon as you remove cookies from oven, cut into 2" lengths.

PEANUT BLOSSOM

½ cup sweet butter
⅓ cup peanut butter
½ cup granulated sugar
½ cup brown sugar
1 egg
1 teaspoon vanilla

1¾ cups all-purpose flour
1 teaspoon baking soda
½ teaspoon salt
1 egg white
Candy kisses

Preheat oven to 375°. Thoroughly grease a cookie sheet. Cream butter and peanut butter. Add the sugars, egg, vanilla, and dry ingredients. Shape dough into balls. Dip each ball in egg white, then in sugar, and place on cookie sheet. Bake for 8 minutes. Remove from oven and top each cookie with a candy kiss pressed firmly into cookie so that it cracks around edges. Return to oven and bake 2 to 5 minutes longer until golden brown.

BOWKNOTS

4 tablespoons sweet butter
½ cup sugar
7 egg yolks
1 teaspoon vanilla
4 tablespoons white wine

1 lemon rind, grated
4 cups all-purpose flour
Shortening
Powdered sugar

Cream butter with sugar. Add yolks, one at a time, then vanilla, wine, and lemon rind. Add flour and knead. Let stand about 15 minutes. Roll dough into an oblong shape, cut into strips 1″ wide and 4″ long, and form into bows.

In a skillet, heat 3″ deep shortening to 380°. Fry the bows until light brown. Sprinkle with powdered sugar.

CHRISTMAS CRULLERS

4 egg yolks	*1½ cups all-purpose flour*
¼ cup powdered sugar	*1 tablespoon brandy*
3 tablespoons sweet butter	*1 tablespoon grated lemon rind*

Mix ingredients and stir until well blended. Chill for about 1 hour. Turn dough onto a floured board. With a pastry wheel, roll out dough until thin and cut it into 3" long strips. Twist each strip round and round. Fry in 3" deep fat at 375° until light brown. Drain on paper towels and sprinkle with powdered sugar.

MARZIPAN COOKIES

A few of these cookies go a long way. They also make a marvelous and professional-looking garnish for a cookie tray.

2 pounds almond paste	*¼ teaspoon salt*
Finely grated orange and	*½ cup unbeaten egg whites*
lemon rind	*1 cup powdered sugar*
1 tablespoon orange brandy	*Food colorings*

Soften the almond paste with flavorings and salt. Mix in the egg whites, add sugar, and continue to cream until smooth. If the mixture is too stiff, very carefully add a little more egg white. The dough should be thick enough to shape into forms.

Divide the dough into small batches. Color one batch red, one batch orange, a small batch green; leave one batch uncolored.

TO MAKE STRAWBERRIES

With the red dough, form little balls. Using both hands, roll each ball into a cone shape resembling a strawberry, then roll in red sugar. Place a stem on top. (Stems are sold in shops selling party goods.)

TO MAKE PEARS

Use plain uncolored dough. Shape into cones, then dip one side in green sugar, the other side in red sugar. Put stem on top.

TO MAKE APPLES

Shape into balls, place a whole clove on one end for the stem. Sprinkle with colored sugars.

TO MAKE PEA PODS

Make a flat disk the size of a quarter from the green dough. Make tiny balls down the center and fold both ends toward the center to enfold the peas.

TO MAKE ORANGES

Make little balls from the orange-colored dough. With a grater, tap the balls around and put a clove in one end.

TO MAKE POTATOES

Roll a little plain dough in small ovals. Make the "eyes" with a little nail. Sprinkle the potato with cocoa or cinnamon.

Let all the marzipan forms dry, then place in colored candy cups to serve. Carefully covered, these can be stored for some time. Should you want these confections to look more glamorous, brush with a gelatin glaze as follows:

GLAZE

6 tablespoons cold water	*1 tablespoon sugar*
1 envelope plain gelatin	*1 tablespoon brandy*

Dissolve ingredients. Set over hot water until thoroughly dissolved. When the mixture is syrupy, brush each cookie form with a pastry brush and let dry in a cool place. This procedure isn't a must but adds to the attractiveness of the product.

PIES

PIE CRUSTS

GRAHAM CRACKER CRUMB CRUST

This recipe makes enough dough to line a 10″ spring-form pan or pie pan.

1½ cups crumbs
¼ cup sugar
¼ cup chopped almonds

1 teaspoon cinnamon
¼ cup melted sweet butter

Combine all ingredients. Press the mixture evenly onto bottom and sides of greased pie pan or spring-form pan. Chill.

MY FAVORITE PIE CRUST

You can use this crust for many kinds of fillings, but it's especially delicious for fruit pies. It is enough for two 9″ crusts, or one pie with top and bottom crust. I prefer not to chill the dough but just to roll it out on a lightly floured board immediately after mixing.

2½ cups all-purpose flour
½ teaspoon salt
½ cup cold sweet butter

½ cup shortening
4 tablespoons cold orange juice

Sift dry ingredients in bowl. Add butter and shortening. Rub with fingertips until it looks pebbly. You can work the dough at this point without fear of overhandling. But at *the next point be cautious:* With a knife, cut orange juice into butter-flour mixture until it forms a ball. Roll out and line a pie pan.

FLAKY PIE CRUST

If you want to make My Favorite Pie Crust dough (see preceding page) into a flakier pastry, roll it out into a rectangle about ⅓″ thick. Cover with 3 tablespoons cold bits of butter. Fold the rectangle across into thirds and turn it on the board so the folded side is facing you. Roll it out, fold in thirds again and roll into final shape.

TENDER PIE PASTRY

This makes two 9″ tender crusts that hold their shape perfectly. You could also use this pastry around meat, as in Beef Wellington.

1½ cups plus 2 tablespoons 　all-purpose flour	¾ cup plus 2 tablespoons 　sweet butter, softened
½ teaspoon salt	2 egg yolks

Sift flour and salt into a large bowl. Make a well in the center and put in it the butter and egg yolks. Mix and blend with fingertips. Add 1 or 2 tablespoons cold water and mix the dough to form a ball. Wrap in waxed paper and chill before using.

SOUR CREAM FLAKY PASTRY

This is a good all-purpose pastry for pies and turnovers. It makes one 9″ crust.

1½ cups all-purpose flour	¼ cup cold sweet butter
1 teaspoon salt	6 tablespoons sour cream

Sift together the flour and salt. Cut in the butter, leaving the mixture in coarse lumps. Cut in the sour cream, a little at a time, using no more than is necessary to hold the dough together. *Add no water*. Roll out the dough in a rectangle and fold it in thirds. Chill the folded dough wrapped in waxed paper for at least 30 minutes before using.

SWEET PIE PASTRY

This recipe is for a 9″ or 10″ pie crust. It can be used for any fruit or cheese pie.

2 cups sifted all-purpose flour
¼ cup sugar
⅛ teaspoon baking powder
5 tablespoons cold sweet
  butter
2 tablespoons vegetable
  shortening, chilled
4 tablespoons ground nuts
1 egg, beaten
1 teaspoon lemon juice

Place flour, sugar, and baking powder in a bowl. With fingertips, rub the butter and shortening into the flour mixture. (Don't be afraid of handling the dough too much.) Add nuts. At this point, be cautious about overmixing. Cut the egg and lemon juice into the dough. If too dry, very carefully add a little more lemon juice.

You can roll out the dough at once on floured waxed paper or chill before rolling.

CHOCOLATE WAFER PIE CRUST

This recipe covers a 9" pie pan.

1½ cups chocolate wafer crumbs
¼ cup sugar
⅓ cup melted sweet butter

Preheat oven to 450°. Thoroughly mix the chocolate crumbs, sugar, and butter. Press the crumbs against bottom and sides of greased pie pan. Bake for 5 minutes. Chill.

DOUBLE BOSTON CREAM PIE

Though this wonderful concoction is always called a pie, it is really a filled cake. Maybe its name came about because it's American as apple pie.

SPONGE CAKE

1¾ cups cake flour, sifted
2 teaspoons baking powder
½ teaspoon salt
8 eggs
1¾ cups superfine sugar
2 teaspoons grated orange rind
1 teaspoon orange flavoring

Preheat oven to 350°. Thoroughly grease four 9" layer-cake pans. Sift flour with baking powder and salt and set aside. Separate eggs, placing whites in a large bowl and yolks in a medium bowl. With electric mixer, beat whites until peaks form, then very gradually add 1 cup sugar, 1 tablespoon at a time.

Beat yolks and add remaining sugar and the orange rind and flavoring until mixture is thick. Fold into egg whites and very carefully fold in the flour, a third at a time. Divide batter into four pans. Bake for 20 to 25 minutes.

FILLING

½ cup sugar	1 teaspoon vanilla
¼ cup all-purpose flour	Grated rind of 1 orange
1½ cups cream	1 teaspoon orange flavoring
4 egg yolks	1 cup heavy cream

In a medium saucepan, combine sugar and flour. Stir in the cream until smooth. Cook over medium heat, stirring until mixture thickens and boils. Remove from heat.

In a small bowl, beat egg yolks slightly. Stir in ½ cup of hot mixture, then pour back into remaining mixture in saucepan and return to heat. Cook, stirring constantly, for 2 minutes longer. Stir in the vanilla and grated orange rind and flavoring. Cool.

Beat cream until stiff and fold into the mixture. Refrigerate.

GLAZE

3 tablespoons cream	2 tablespoons sweet butter
1 ounce unsweetened chocolate	¾ cup powdered sugar

Heat cream in a small saucepan. Stir in the chocolate and butter. When melted, add powdered sugar and stir until smooth.

Spread 3 cake layers with filling and top with fourth layer. Spread glaze on top, allowing to run down the sides. Decorate with chocolate curls if you like.

BASIC CREAM FILLING FOR CREAM PIES

2 cups heavy or light cream ½ cup all-purpose flour
6 egg yolks ½ teaspoon salt
1 cup sugar

Put all ingredients in top of double boiler. Mix and cook until thick. Flavor according to the kind of pie you're making.

BLUEBERRY CREAM PIE

1 9″ crumb crust 2 cups sour cream
  or baked pie crust (see pages 3 tablespoons sweet sherry
  173--75) ½ teaspoon almond extract
1 can commercial blueberry Almond slivers, toasted
  pie filling
Basic Cream Filling (above)

Into a baked pie shell, spoon half of the blueberry filling. To the basic cream filling, add sour cream, 2 tablespoons sweet sherry and almond extract. Pour over the blueberry layer. Refrigerate for 2 hours to set.

Add remaining sherry to the rest of the blueberry filling. Pour over the cream filling and sprinkle with almond slivers.

PECAN LEMON PIE

1 9" unbaked pie crust
  (see pages 173–75)
Basic Cream Filling (page 178)
2 tablespoons sweet butter
1/3 cup dark brown sugar
1 egg
1/4 cup light corn syrup
1 teaspoon vanilla

1/2 teaspoon grated lemon rind
1/4 teaspoon salt
1/2 cup chopped pecans
1/3 cup chopped dates
2 cups heavy cream
Grated rind of 2 lemons
2 teaspoons lemon juice

Prepare pie crust and basic cream filling. Preheat oven to 400°. Beat butter and brown sugar until smooth with an electric mixer. Add egg, corn syrup, vanilla, lemon rind, and salt. Beat until well blended. Mix in the chopped pecans and dates. Pour mixture into pie shell. Bake for 25 minutes, or until filling is firm. Cool.

Whip cream and add 1 cup to basic cream filling along with grated rind and lemon juice. Pour over the baked pecan filling and pipe the remaining cup of sweetened whipped cream over the top with a pastry tube.

CHERRY CREAM PIE

1 9" crumb crust
  or baked pie crust (see pages
  173–75)
Basic Cream Filling (page 178)

2 cups heavy cream, whipped
1/2 teaspoon almond extract
1 can commercial cherry pie filling

Prepare pie crust. Into the basic cream filling, mix 1 cup whipped cream and almond extract. Pour into pie shell and top with cherry filling. Top with remaining whipped cream, either piped on with pastry tube or artistically spread.

CRÈME DE CACAO PIE

CRUST

1½ cups finely crushed
chocolate wafers

¼ cup sugar
½ cup melted sweet butter

Preheat oven to 375°. Butter bottom and sides of a 9″ pie pan. In a bowl, combine all ingredients. Press the mixture over the bottom and sides of pan and bake for 5 minutes. Cool.

FILLING

2 teaspoons gelatin
1⅓ cups heavy cream
4 egg yolks

¼ cup sugar
⅓ cup brandy
⅓ cup dark crème de cacao

In a bowl, sprinkle gelatin over ⅓ cup heavy cream and soften for 5 minutes. Stir the gelatin over hot water until dissolved; let it cool but *do not* let it set.

Beat egg yolks until frothy, gradually beating in the sugar. Continue to beat for several minutes or until the mixture ribbons when the beater is lifted.

Stir in the brandy, crème de cacao, and gelatin. Chill the mixture until slightly thickened. Whip remaining heavy cream and fold it in. Pour mixture into pie shell. Put pie in the freezer compartment of the refrigerator until frozen. Remove it about 10 minutes before serving. Pipe additional whipped cream rosettes on top. Or sprinkle chocolate curls on top.

HOLIDAY EGGNOG PIE

1 9" Graham Cracker Crumb
 Crust (page 173) or Chocolate
 Wafer Pie
 Crust (page 176)
1 tablespoon unflavored
 gelatin
¼ cup cold water
⅓ cup sugar

2 tablespoons cornstarch
⅛ teaspoon salt
2 cups commercial eggnog
1½ squares unsweetened
 chocolate, melted
1 teaspoon vanilla
2 tablespoons rum
1 cup heavy cream, whipped

Prepare pie crust. Sprinkle gelatin on water to soften. In a saucepan mix together the sugar, cornstarch, and salt. Gradually stir in the eggnog. Cook in top of double boiler, stirring constantly until thickened. Remove from heat and stir in the softened gelatin until dissolved. Divide filling in half. Add melted chocolate and vanilla to one half. Set aside. Allow remaining half to cool and then add the rum and the whipped cream.

Pour the rum-flavored mixture into the pie shell, then pour the chocolate mixture on top and finish as follows:

TOPPING

1 cup heavy cream, whipped   ¼ cup rum
¼ cup powdered sugar

Beat all ingredients together and pipe the top of the pie with a pastry tube. Sprinkle with chocolate curls or place commercial chocolate stars around rim of pie. Chill for several hours before serving.

CHOCOLATE ANGEL PIE

PECAN MERINGUE PIE SHELL

3 egg whites   ¾ cup sugar
⅛ teaspoon salt   ½ teaspoon vanilla
¼ teaspoon cream of tartar   ⅓ cup chopped pecans

Preheat oven to 275°. Thoroughly grease bottom and sides of 9″ pie pan. Combine egg whites, salt, and cream of tartar. Beat until soft peaks form, then very gradually add the sugar and beat until stiff. Add vanilla. Spread over the bottom and sides of pie pan. Build up the sides. Sprinkle the chopped nuts on bottom of shell and bake for 1 hour. Cool.

FILLING

¾ cup semisweet chocolate   1 teaspoon vanilla
    pieces   ⅛ teaspoon salt
¼ cup hot milk   1 cup heavy cream, whipped

Melt chocolate pieces in a bowl over hot water or put them in a pan and place in a 325° oven for 5 minutes. Add hot milk, vanilla, and salt. Stir until smooth. Cool and fold in the whipped cream.

Pour the filling into the meringue shell. Chill for 4 hours or overnight. Spread a thin layer of additional whipped cream on top before serving if desired.

PRALINE PUMPKIN PIE

PRALINE SHELL

⅓ cup finely chopped pecans
⅓ cup brown sugar
2 tablespoons sweet butter,
   softened

1 unbaked 9″ pie crust
   (see pages 173–74) chilled

Blend pecans with sugar and butter. Press gently with the back of a spoon into bottom of pie shell.

FILLING AND MERINGUE

3 whole eggs
2 eggs, separated
1 cup canned pumpkin
½ cup brown sugar
1½ cups heavy cream
¼ cup rum

½ teaspoon salt
1 teaspoon cinnamon
¼ teaspoon ground cloves
¼ teaspoon ginger
¼ teaspoon mace
2 tablespoons granulated sugar

Preheat oven to 400°. Blend all ingredients except egg whites and granulated sugar.

Pour into pie shell and bake for about 50 minutes.

Meanwhile, make the meringue: beat egg whites until stiff, adding sugar while beating. Remove pie from oven, cover with the meringue, and return to 425° oven to brown. Watch carefully.

LEMON MERINGUE PIE

This is a nice tart pie and not too wicked in calories because there is no thickening added.

1 baked pie crust or 1 crumb crust (see pages 173–75)

FILLING

10 eggs, separated *1 cup fresh lemon juice*
2½ cups sugar *Grated rind of 1 lemon*
¼ teaspoon salt

Beat 10 egg yolks and 4 egg whites with 2 cups sugar, salt, and lemon juice. Place in top of double boiler and stir with a wooden spoon until custard is thick. Remove from heat and add grated rind.

Beat remaining egg whites until stiff and very gradually add remaining sugar. Continue to beat until thick. Fold half of the meringue into the custard.

Pour into the baked pie crust or crumb crust, cover with remaining meringue, and put under the broiler until lightly browned.

BLACK BOTTOM PIE

CRUST

1 cup crushed ginger snaps, chocolate wafers or graham crackers	4 tablespoons melted sweet butter
	2 tablespoons brown sugar
	1 teaspoon cinnamon

Thoroughly grease a 9″ or 10″ pie pan. Combine all ingredients. Press the mixture onto bottom and sides of pan.

FILLING

2 cups half-and-half cream	1 tablespoon gelatin
4 eggs, separated	1 tablespoon cold water
2 tablespoons cornstarch	6 tablespoons rum
1 cup sugar	¼ teaspoon cream of tartar
Dash of salt	1 cup heavy cream, whipped
2 squares chocolate, melted	Shaved chocolate
1 teaspoon vanilla	

Scald the half-and-half cream and very slowly add to beaten egg yolks. Combine cornstarch with ½ cup sugar and add to cream mixture. Cook in top of double boiler, stirring constantly until thick. Add salt and remove from heat. Put 1 cup of the custard mixture in a bowl and add melted chocolate and vanilla. Set aside.

185

Dissolve gelatin in water and add to remaining hot custard. Add 4 tablespoons rum. Beat egg whites until stiff. Gradually add remaining sugar and cream of tartar, beating until stiff. Fold into the custard and pour into the pie shell. Pour the reserved chocolate custard on top and cover with whipped cream, to which the remaining rum has been added. Top with shaved chocolate.

GRASSHOPPER PIE

CHOCOLATE SHELL

½ cup semisweet chocolate   3 cups toasted Rice Krispies
   pieces

Thoroughly grease a 9″ pie pan. Melt chocolate in a double boiler over hot water. Add Rice Krispies and stir gently until evenly coated. Pour mixture into a pie pan. Spread evenly over bottom and sides. Refrigerate.

FILLING

¾ cup sugar   1¾ cups cream
3 tablespoons cornstarch   ¼ cup crème de menthe
¼ teaspoon salt   ½ teaspoon peppermint flavoring
3 egg yolks   Green food coloring

Combine all ingredients in a heavy 2-quart saucepan. Cook until thick. Cool. Pour into pie shell.

TOPPING

1 cup heavy cream, whipped　　2 tablespoons sugar
2 tablespoons crème de menthe　　Semisweet chocolate bar

Combine whipped cream with crème de menthe and sugar.

Cover pie and decorate with curls, scraped with vegetable peeler from chocolate bar.

RHUBARB-PINEAPPLE CHIFFON PIE

2 cups diced rhubarb
½ cup pineapple juice
¾ cup plus 4 tablespoons
　sugar
2 eggs, separated
¼ teaspoon salt
½ teaspoon mace

1 tablespoon unflavored gelatin
¼ cup cold water
¾ cup crushed pineapple,
　well drained
1 cup heavy cream
1 Graham Cracker Crumb Crust
　recipe (page 173)

Cook rhubarb with pineapple juice and ¾ cup sugar in covered pan until rhubarb is barely tender. Add a little of the hot rhubarb sauce to slightly beaten egg yolks. Combine with rest of rhubarb sauce. Add salt and mace and cook in top of double boiler until thickened. Soak gelatin in water and add to hot mixture, stirring until dissolved. Chill until mixture begins to thicken. Fold in the pineapple. Beat egg whites, gradually adding remaining sugar, until stiff. Whip the cream and fold in half of it. Pour into pie crust and chill for several hours. Spread with the rest of the whipped cream, or put the whipped cream in a pastry bag with a star tube and decorate the top.

PUMPKIN RUM PIE

Line a 9" pie pan with unbaked pie crust (see pages 173–74) and fill as follows:

FILLING

3 eggs	*1 teaspoon cinnamon*
½ cup brown sugar	*½ teaspoon ground cloves*
½ teaspoon salt	*¼ teaspoon mace*
1½ cups heavy cream	*1 cup heavy cream, whipped*
1 cup canned pumpkin	*1 tablespoon rum*
¼ cup rum	

Preheat oven to 400°. Mix all ingredients together except whipped cream and rum, and pour into pie shell. Bake for 35 minutes. Test the filling by sticking a silver knife in the center—if it comes out clean the pie is ready. When entirely cooled, pipe sweetened whipped cream, flavored with rum, all over the top.

FRENCH UPSIDE DOWN APPLE TART

½ cup sweet butter	*½ cup sugar*
6 large tart apples, cored	*1 teaspoon grated lemon rind*
and thinly sliced	

Thoroughly butter an 8″ x 8″ baking pan. Melt butter in a large skillet. Add apples, sugar, and lemon rind. Toss apples in butter until softened. Transfer to another pan. Let cool.

CARAMEL

½ cup sugar
3 tablespoons water
Pinch of cream of tartar

1 cup whipped cream, sweetened
1 tablespoon rum or brandy

Preheat oven to 425°. Lightly butter a 9″ pie pan. In a heavy skillet, cook sugar, water, and cream of tartar over medium heat. Wash down any undissolved sugar that clings to the sides of the pan with a brush dipped in cold water. Cook until caramel mixture is golden and pour into a 9″ pie pan (the caramel should coat the bottom evenly). Let it set, then arrange a layer of overlapping circles of apple slices over the caramel. Cover with pie dough of choice: either the Sour Cream Flaky Pastry (page 174) or the Flaky Pie Crust (page 174). Bake on a baking sheet for about 45 minutes. If you prefer, you can use a thin sheet of Basic Sweet Dough (page 227) instead of pie crust and bake in 350° oven for about 35 minutes. Let cool for 30 minutes and invert on serving dish. Serve with whipped cream sweetened and flavored to taste.

CHEESE
CAKES

MUNICH CHEESE CAKE

This cheese cake is very unusual.

CRUST

1 cup all-purpose flour
¼ teaspoon salt
3 tablespoons sugar

½ cup sweet butter
1 egg yolk

Butter bottom and sides of a 9″ spring-form pan. In a mixing bowl, sift together flour, salt, and sugar. Add butter and blend with fingertips until mixture looks like coarse meal. Cut in the egg yolk. Press the mixture onto bottom and sides of pan.

FILLING

12 ounces cream cheese,
   softened
2 eggs

½ cup sugar
¼ teaspoon salt
1 vanilla bean, split

Preheat oven to 350°. Beat cream cheese, adding eggs, sugar, salt, and the seeds scraped from inside the vanilla bean.

Spread the mixture over the crust and bake for 35 minutes. Let cool on wire rack.

FIRST TOPPING

1 cup poppy seeds	½ cup heavy cream
¾ cup golden raisins, soaked and drained	Grated rind of 1 lemon
¾ cup sugar	1 vanilla bean, split

Whirl poppy seeds, a few at a time, in a blender, until they are reduced to a coarse powder. Put in saucepan and stir in the raisins, sugar, cream, lemon rind, and the seeds scraped from inside the vanilla bean. Cook the mixture over low heat, stirring frequently, for about 20 minutes. Let cool.

Spread the mixture over the cheese cake. For additional flavor, top as follows:

SECOND TOPPING

6 tablespoons all-purpose flour	6 tablespoons brown sugar
	¼ cup sweet butter

Mix flour and brown sugar together. Cut in the butter until the mixture turns into coarse crumbs. Sprinkle over the cheese cake and set it under the broiler about 6″ from heat. Broil for about 3 minutes, or until topping is brown and crisp. Watch carefully so it doesn't burn.

Cool the cake completely. It can be chilled, but let it return to almost room temperature before serving. Cut in thin wedges.

GERMAN CHEESE CAKE

CRUST

1 cup plus 1 tablespoon
  all-purpose flour
¼ teaspoon salt
1 teaspoon baking powder

2 egg yolks
¼ cup sugar
1 tablespoon milk
¼ cup butter, cut into small pieces

Preheat oven to 325°. Lightly flour a 9″ spring-form cake pan. Into a bowl, sift 1 cup flour, salt, and baking powder. In a separate bowl, beat egg yolks, sugar, and milk together.

With fingertips, rub butter into flour mixture. Add the yolk mixture to the flour and stir until well blended.

On a lightly floured board roll out two-thirds of the dough and line the pan. Stir 1 tablespoon flour into remaining dough and form into a narrow 14″ roll. Place around outer edge of dough base. Press against the sides of the pan to form a rim about an inch high. Prick the dough and bake for 15 minutes. Cool.

FILLING

1 pound cream cheese,
  softened
2 eggs, separated
¾ cup golden raisins

Grated peel of 1 lemon
Basic Cream Filling (page 178)
2 tablespoons sugar

Preheat oven to 350°. Beat cheese until creamy. Add egg yolks, raisins, and lemon peel and add mixture to the basic cream filling. Beat egg whites until peaks form. Add sugar, continue to beat until stiff, and carefully fold the whites into the creamy mixture.

Pour filling into crust and bake for about 1 hour, or until almost set. It will appear soft in the center but it will set after cooling. Sprinkle with powdered sugar when cold.

LEMON-TOPPED CHEESE CAKE

CRUMB LINING CRUST

1½ cups graham cracker
   crumbs
⅓ cup sweet butter

3 tablespoons sugar
1 teaspoon cinnamon

Grease bottom and sides of a 9″ spring-form pan. Blend together all ingredients and press onto bottom and sides of pan.

FILLING

1½ pounds cream cheese,
   softened
1 cup sugar

1 tablespoon vanilla
6 eggs
3 tablespoons all-purpose flour

Preheat oven to 350°. Blend cream cheese with sugar and vanilla. Beat eggs until thick and add flour. Gradually add to cheese mixture. Pour into crust and bake for about 25 to 30 minutes. Cool. Remove sides of spring-form pan and cover with topping.

TOPPING

⅔ cup sugar

3 tablespoons cornstarch

¼ teaspoon salt

¾ cup boiling water

3 egg yolks, beaten

2 tablespoons sweet butter

3 tablespoons lemon juice

2 tablespoons grated lemon rind

Mix sugar, cornstarch, and salt. Slowly add to boiling water and cook, stirring frequently, until thick and smooth. Add some of the hot mixture to egg yolks, then add the rest of it along with the butter. Cook 2 minutes longer. Remove from heat and blend in the lemon juice and rind. Cool well before pouring on cooled cheese cake.

ORANGE CHEESE PIE WITH APRICOTS

GRAHAM CRACKER CRUST

1½ cups ground graham
    crackers

1 teaspoon cinnamon

½ cup brown sugar

½ cup sweet butter, softened

Preheat oven to 350°. Butter a 9″ pie pan. Blend all ingredients thoroughly and press into pan. Bake for 10 minutes. Cool.

FILLING AND GLAZE

8 ounces cream cheese

1 can sweetened condensed
  milk

⅓ cup lemon juice

1 teaspoon orange flavoring

8 canned whole peeled
  apricots, drained and juice
  reserved

¼ cup sugar

2 tablespoons cornstarch

¼ teaspoon salt

½ cup apricot juice

½ cup orange juice

Beat cream cheese until fluffy. Gradually add the milk, blending until smooth. Add lemon juice and orange flavoring.

Pour into baked crust and chill for 3 hours. Arrange apricots on top.

In a small saucepan, mix sugar, cornstarch, salt, apricot juice and orange juice. Mix well and cook until thick and shiny. Cool.

Cover the apricots with the glaze and chill the cake again for 1 hour.

STRAWBERRY CHEESE PIE

CRUST

1½ cups fine graham
  cracker crumbs

⅓ cup melted sweet butter

2 tablespoons brown sugar

1 tablespoon cinnamon

Preheat oven to 350°. Thoroughly butter a 9″ pie pan. Combine all ingredients and press onto sides and bottom of pan. Bake for 10 minutes. Remove from oven and let cool.

FILLING

2 cups fresh hulled
    strawberries or 1 8-ounce
    bag whole frozen berries
1/3 cup granulated sugar
1 tablespoon unflavored
    gelatin

1/4 cup cold water
1 cup creamed cottage cheese,
    sieved
1 cup sour cream
1/2 cup powdered sugar
1 tablespoon lemon juice

Sprinkle berries with granulated sugar and let stand for about 20 minutes. Soak gelatin in cold water and then place over low heat until dissolved. Drain the juice from the strawberries, add 1 tablespoon of the gelatin mixture and mix well. Pour over the strawberries. Chill for at least 30 minutes before spooning half of the berry mixture into the pie shell. Chill.

Add remaining gelatin to sieved cottage cheese (at room temperature). Combine with sour cream, powdered sugar, and lemon juice. Mix well and carefully spoon over the layer of strawberries in the pie shell. Chill for several hours. Just before serving, spoon remaining strawberries on top of the cheese mixture.

CHOCOLATE CHEESE CAKE

This makes a large cake. Cut the recipe in half if you like.

CRUST

½ cup sweet butter

2 tablespoons sugar

2 hard-cooked egg yolks,
  mashed

1 teaspoon brandy

1 teaspoon vanilla

1 raw egg yolk

1 cup sifted all-purpose flour

¼ teaspoon salt

Thoroughly grease a 9″ spring-form pan. Cream butter and sugar. Add brandy and vanilla to the yolks and add to creamed mixture. Blend in the raw yolk, flour, and salt. Pat the dough onto sides and bottom of pan.

FILLING

16 ounces sweet cooking
  chocolate

2½ pounds cream cheese

1½ cups sugar

8 eggs, separated

4 cups heavy cream

1 cup all-purpose flour

3 teaspoons vanilla

Shaved chocolate

Chopped pecans

Preheat oven to 400°. Melt chocolate in top of double boiler over hot water. Remove from heat and cool slightly. Mix cream cheese with half of the sugar and beat in the yolks. Fold in the melted chocolate. Beat whites until stiff and add remaining sugar, 1 tablespoon at a time, until well blended and very stiff. Whip 2 cups cream until stiff and pour over the egg white mixture. Add cream cheese mixture. Sprinkle the flour on top, add vanilla, and fold all ingredients together very gently.

Pour the mixture into the crust. If the filling reaches the rim of the pan, put a 5" strip of greased foil around it and tie with heavy string—this will prevent the filling from spilling over. Bake for 15 minutes and then reduce heat to 350° and continue baking for 1 hour and 15 minutes. Turn off heat and allow cake to remain in oven with door closed for 3 hours. The cake may crack, but this is all right. Chill cake and remove from spring form. Whip remaining cream and spread over top and sides. Decorate with chocolate shavings on top and chopped pecans around sides.

MARBLE CHEESE CAKE

CRUMB CRUST

1 cup chocolate cookie crumbs   *1 teaspoon cinnamon*
2 tablespoons melted sweet
  butter

Preheat oven to 350°. Grease bottom of 8" spring-form pan. Mix all ingredients and press onto bottom of pan. Bake for 5 to 8 minutes. Cool.

FILLING

2 tablespoons unflavored
   gelatin
1 cup sugar
3 eggs, separated
1⅓ cups milk

2 teaspoons vanilla
1 pound cream cheese, at
   room temperature
1 cup heavy cream, whipped
1 cup semisweet chocolate pieces

Mix gelatin and ¾ cup sugar together in a saucepan. Beat yolks and 1 cup milk together. Stir into the gelatin mixture and place over low heat. Stir constantly until gelatin dissolves and mixture thickens slightly, about 5 minutes.

Remove from heat. Stir in the vanilla and chill, stirring occasionally until the mixture is thoroughly cool.

Cream the cream cheese in a large bowl and gradually blend in the gelatin mixture. Beat egg whites until stiff and gradually add remaining sugar, beating until very stiff. Fold into the gelatin mixture and then fold in the whipped cream.

In a saucepan, melt chocolate pieces with remaining milk over very low heat. Cool. Add chocolate to one-third of the gelatin mixture. Alternate white and chocolate mixtures in prepared crust and lightly swirl with knife to marbleize. Chill 3 to 4 hours until firm. Remove sides of spring form to serve.

If you want to decorate the top, you can scrape a bar of semisweet chocolate with vegetable cutter to make curls.

MARBLEIZED CHEESE CAKE

You have a choice of two kinds of crust for this cake.

FIRST CRUST

½ cup sweet butter
2 tablespoons sugar
2 egg yolks

2 hard-cooked egg yolks
1 teaspoon vanilla
1 cup sifted all-purpose flour

Thoroughly grease a 9″ spring-form pan. Cream butter and sugar. Add the raw and cooked yolks mashed with vanilla. Gradually add flour. Chill for about 1 hour and then pat onto bottom and sides of pan.

SECOND CRUST

1 package chocolate wafers
¼ cup sweet butter

½ teaspoon cinnamon

Crumb the chocolate wafers. Mix with butter and cinnamon and sprinkle into greased spring-form pan.

FILLING

2½ pounds cream cheese
1 teaspoon vanilla
5 eggs
2 egg yolks
½ cup heavy cream

1 ¾ cups sugar
5 tablespoons all-purpose flour
4 ounces semisweet chocolate, melted
Powdered sugar

Preheat oven to 375°. Beat cream cheese until fluffy. Add vanilla, eggs and yolks, and cream. Gradually beat in sugar and flour.

Pour mixture onto the crust and gradually pour in the melted chocolate. Run a knife through the cream cheese batter. Bake for about 1 hour and 15 minutes. When cake is cooled, sprinkle with powdered sugar or glaze with the following:

CHOCOLATE GLAZE

4 ounces semisweet chocolate   *2 tablespoons sweet butter*

Melt chocolate with butter in the top of a double boiler.

PUMPKIN CHEESE CAKE

CRUST

¾ cup graham cracker crumbs   *1 teaspoon cinnamon*
3 tablespoons melted sweet   *2 tablespoons brown sugar*
*   butter*

Preheat oven to 350°. Thoroughly grease a 9″ spring-form pan. Combine all ingredients and line the bottom and sides of the pan.

FILLING

2 pounds cream cheese,
  softened
1½ cups plus 2 tablespoons
  sugar
5 whole eggs

¼ cup all-purpose flour
1 1-pound can of pumpkin purée
2 teaspoons pumpkin pie spice
2 tablespoons rum
1 cup heavy cream, whipped

Cream the cream cheese until fluffy. Gradually add 1½ cups sugar and the eggs, one at a time, beating after each addition. Gradually add flour, mixed with spice, and pumpkin. Add rum.

Pour into the crust and bake for about 1 hour and 45 minutes, or until the center feels quite firm when touched.

When entirely cooled, cover top with whipped cream sweetened with 2 tablespoons sugar. Add 1 teaspoon rum if you like. Pipe with star-tipped pastry bag. Sprinkle with toasted chopped almonds or pecan pieces (this is optional).

COGNAC CHEESE CAKE

CRUST

1 cup fine graham cracker
   crumbs
2 tablespoons melted sweet
   butter

2 tablespoons sugar
½ teaspoon cinnamon

Thoroughly butter the bottom and sides of a 9″ spring-form pan. Mix all ingredients together. Press the crumbs lightly against bottom and sides of pan.

FILLING

2½ cups heavy cream
2 pounds cream cheese
12 egg yolks
2 cups sugar
8 tablespoons cognac

2 tablespoons grated orange rind
6 egg whites
8 tablespoons all-purpose flour
Powdered sugar

Preheat oven to 400°. Gradually add cream to cream cheese, beating the mixture thoroughly. Add flour. Beat yolks with sugar until light, and add cognac and orange rind. Beat until smooth. Beat egg whites until stiff and gradually fold into the cheese mixture together with the flour.

Pour into the crust and bake for 15 minutes. To make sure the filling won't spill over, tie a 5" strip of greased foil around the rim of the pan with heavy string. Reduce heat to 350° and finish baking for about 1 hour and 15 minutes, or until cake feels solid when you press your finger against the middle. Let cool. Remove the sides of the pan and sprinkle with powdered sugar.

EMILIO'S CHEESE CAKE (CRUSTLESS)

2 pounds cream cheese
1½ cups sugar
¼ pound sweet butter,
    softened
¼ cup cornstarch

Juice and grated rind of 2 lemons
6 eggs
2 cups heavy cream
1 teaspoon vanilla

Preheat oven to 350°. Thoroughly grease or spray a 9" springform pan. Beat cream cheese thoroughly. Still beating slowly and thoroughly, add sugar, and then the butter, starch, lemon juice and rinds, eggs, cream, and vanilla. Beat until well blended.

Pour the batter into the pan. If the filling reaches the rim of the pan, tie a 5" strip of greased foil around it with heavy string—this will keep the filling from spilling over. Bake for about 1½ hours or until nicely browned—at this point, it is done even if it feels soft to the touch. Don't worry about it. Overcooking will make the cake granulate. Take it out of the oven and let it cool (it will solidify as it cools).

Place the cake on a serving plate. If you wish to further enhance the cake, cover with a fruit topping.

STRAWBERRY TOPPING (optional)

2 pints fresh hulled
   strawberries
½ cup plus 2 tablespoons
   cold water

1 cup sugar
2 tablespoons cornstarch
Juice of 1 lemon

Crush ½ pint of the berries with sugar and water. Put on the stove to boil. Mix the starch with 2 tablespoons cold water and add to boiling mixture, stirring constantly until mixture is clear and thick. Add lemon juice.

    Put remaining uncooked berries on the cake and pour the cooked berry glaze over the berries.

TOM AND JERRY CHEESE CAKE

CRUST

1 cup vanilla wafer crumbs
¼ cup melted sweet butter

1 teaspoon cinnamon

Preheat oven to 325°. Thoroughly grease a 9″ spring-form pan. Combine ingredients and press onto bottom of pan. Bake for 8 to 10 minutes. Cool.

FILLING

4 cups miniature
   marshmallows
⅓ cup orange juice
1 pound cream cheese,
   softened

1 teaspoon rum flavoring
1 cup heavy cream, whipped
Maraschino cherries with stems
Pecan halves

Melt marshmallows with orange juice over low flame. Stir until smooth, then chill until thickened. Combine cream cheese and rum flavoring, and beat until light and fluffy. Whip in the marshmallow mixture and fold in the whipped cream.

   Pour into the crust, chill, and garnish with maraschino cherries and pecan halves. Remove sides of spring form to serve.

HOLLYWOOD CHEESE CAKE

Remove all ingredients for this cake from the refrigerator 1 hour before making it. This cake can be kept in the refrigerator for three or four days.

CRUST

1 teaspoon unsalted shortening
1¼ cups crushed graham
   crackers

1 teaspoon cinnamon
¼ cup sugar
¼ cup melted sweet butter

Grease a 9″ spring-form pan with shortening. Sift crumbs with cinnamon, combine with sugar and butter, and cover sides and bottom of pan.

FILLING

2 pounds cream cheese   *6 eggs*
1 cup sugar   *2 teaspoons vanilla*

Preheat oven to 375°. Cream the cheese. Add sugar, eggs and vanilla and beat until smooth. Pour into crumb-lined pan and bake for about 40 minutes. Remove and let cool for about 15 minutes.

TOPPING

1½ pints sour cream   *2 teaspoons vanilla*
½ cup sugar

Raise heat to 425°. Mix sour cream, sugar and vanilla until well blended.
   Spread over the filling and bake for about 10 minutes. Remove from oven and let stand at room temperature for about 5 hours before serving.

VERY LOW CALORIE CHEESE CAKE

CRUST

¼ cup sugar   *⅓ cup sweet butter*
1 cup all-purpose flour   *1 egg yolk*

Preheat oven to 300°. Grease an 8″ spring-form pan. Combine sugar, flour and butter and crumble with the fingertips. Stir in the egg yolk. Work vigorously with your hands into a ball. Press onto bottom of pan and bake for 30 minutes. Let cool.

FILLING

1 pint large-curd cottage	*1 egg white*
cheese	*1 teaspoon grated lemon peel*
1 cup sugar	*1 teaspoon lemon juice*
1 tablespoon all-purpose flour	*1 teaspoon vanilla*
¼ teaspoon salt	*8 ounces strawberry yogurt*
3 eggs	

Preheat oven to 350°. In a blender, combine the cottage cheese, sugar, flour, salt, whole eggs and egg white. Whirl until smooth. Stir in the lemon peel and juice and vanilla.

Pour into the crust and bake for about 1 hour, or until set. Remove and chill for about 2 hours. Spread yogurt on top to serve.

CAKE
ROLLS

SPONGE CAKE USED FOR CREAM ROLLS

9 large eggs, separated
1 teaspoon cream of tartar
1½ cups sugar
1 teaspoon orange flavoring

Grated rind of 1 orange
1 cup potato starch (sometimes
   called potato flour)
½ teaspoon salt

Preheat oven to 375°. Thoroughly grease and line with brown paper a 13″ x 17″ jelly-roll pan. Beat egg whites until foamy. Add cream of tartar and very gradually, 1 tablespoon at a time, ¾ cup sugar. Continue beating until thick and shiny. Set aside.

Beat egg yokes until thick. Add remaining sugar, orange flavoring and rind, and continue beating until thick. Beat in the potato starch mixed with salt until the batter is smooth. Fold part of egg whites into the yolk mixture. Then very carefully fold this mixture into the remaining egg whites.

Pour the mixture into the pan and bake for about 20 minutes. Remove from oven and let cool slightly. Turn out onto sugar-sprinkled foil or waxed paper and roll up like a jelly roll. Let cool completely before unrolling and filling.

LEMON ROLL

This tart and light dessert is delectable after a heavy meal.

CAKE

4 eggs, separated
1/4 cup sugar
1/4 cup all-purpose flour

1/4 cup cornstarch
1/2 teaspoon vanilla
1/2 teaspoon grated lemon rind

Preheat oven to 400°. Butter an 11" x 16" jelly-roll pan and line it with waxed paper. In a bowl, beat egg whites until frothy. Add sugar, 1 table-spoon at a time and beat until stiff. In another bowl, beat yolks well, add one-quarter of the whites and fold them in gently but thoroughly. Pour the yolk mixture onto the remaining whites and sift flour and cornstarch on top. Fold the mixture together, adding vanilla and grated lemon rind, until there are no traces of white. Turn batter into pan and spread evenly. Bake for 10 minutes, or until lightly browned. Loosen the waxed paper and invert the cake onto a baking sheet sprinkled with powdered sugar. Let the cake cool and peel off the waxed paper. Roll up until ready to fill.

FILLING

1 cup sweet butter
2/3 cup plus 2 tablespoons
    sugar
1/4 cup water
1/4 cup plus 1 tablespoon
    lemon juice

1/4 teaspoon cream of tartar
4 eggs, separated
1 tablespoon gelatin
1 1/2 teaspoons grated lemon rind
Toasted and chopped blanched
    almonds (optional)

216

In a heavy saucepan, combine butter, ⅔ cup sugar, water, ¼ cup lemon juice, cream of tartar, and egg yolks. Stir the mixture over low heat until it thickens enough to coat a spoon. Dissolve gelatin in remaining lemon juice and pour into hot mixture. Remove pan from heat and add grated rind. Pour the mixture into a bowl and let cool. Beat egg whites gradually, adding remaining sugar, and continue to beat until stiff. Carefully fold into the yolk mixture.

Unroll the sponge cake. Spread it with most of the filling and roll tightly, lifting it with the waxed paper and finishing with the seam down. Dust the roll with powdered sugar. Spread the rest of the filling on top of the roll and sprinkle with chocolate curls made by scraping a chocolate bar with a vegetable peeler. The sides can be sprinkled with toasted and chopped blanched almonds. Refrigerate until ready to serve.

CHOCOLATE CREAM ROLL

CAKE

¾ cup sugar

½ cup sifted cake flour

¼ cup sifted cocoa

7 eggs, separated

⅛ teaspoon salt

1 teaspoon cream of tartar

1 teaspoon vanilla

Preheat oven to 400°. Line a 12" x 18" pan with heavy paper. Sift sugar, then sift combined flour and cocoa three times. Beat egg whites, adding salt, cream of tartar and, gradually, ¼ cup sugar, beating until stiff. Set aside.

Beat yolks until thick and lemon-colored, gradually adding the remaining sugar and vanilla. Fold into egg whites and carefully fold in the flour and cocoa. *Do not overmix.* Pour into pan and bake for 12 to 15 minutes. Remove from oven and turn out on a large piece of brown paper sprinkled with powdered sugar. Roll up the cake and let it cool completely.

FILLING

½ cup sugar	*2 cups heavy cream*
1 teaspoon vanilla	*Chopped nuts or chocolate curls*

Whip cream until stiff and add sugar and vanilla.

Unroll cake and spread with whipped cream mixture. Roll it up again and spread some of the cream on top. Sprinkle with either chopped nuts or chocolate curls (made by scraping a semisweet chocolate bar with vegetable peeler). Refrigerate until ready to serve.

OTHER FILLINGS

The roll can be filled with 1 quart peppermint ice cream or with whipped cream flavored with rum or with a mocha filling (to the whipped cream filling, add 1 tablespoon instant coffee, 2 tablespoons cocoa, and ½ cup sugar).

CHOCOLATE MOCHA RUM ROLL

Expensive—yes. But oh, so good!

1 rolled Sponge Cake
    (page 215)
1 cup sugar
¾ cup black coffee
½ teaspoon cream of tartar
10 egg yolks

2 cups sweet butter
½ cup rum
½ cup cocoa
Dash of salt
2 cups heavy cream

In a small saucepan, mix together the sugar, coffee, and cream of tartar and stir over medium heat until dissolved. Wash down the sides of the pan with a brush dipped in hot water. Let boil (do not stir) until candy thermometer registers 238°, or a drop of syrup tested in cold water forms a soft ball.

In a large bowl, beat the yolks until thick. When the syrup reaches the right temperature, remove from heat and pour the syrup in a very fine stream onto the thick yolks, continuing to beat until mixture has partially cooled. Add butter while still beating and blend thoroughly. Gradually add rum, cocoa, and salt and beat until thick. Whip the cream and set aside.

Unroll the cooled sponge cake. Spread with half of the chocolate rum filling and spread over this a layer of half the whipped cream. Roll up the cake like a jelly roll. Spread the outside with the remaining filling, and then with the remaining whipped cream. Sprinkle with chocolate curls.

NOTE: Save the egg whites for angel food cake or meringues.

GINGER WALNUT ROLL WITH MOLASSES CREAM

CAKE

7 eggs, separated
1/3 cup sugar
1/2 teaspoon salt

3/4 cup ground walnuts, pecans
or almonds
2 teaspoons ground ginger

Preheat oven to 350°. Line an 11" x 6" jelly-roll pan with greased waxed paper. Beat egg yolks until frothy, gradually adding sugar. Continue to beat the mixture for several minutes, or until it ribbons when beater is lifted. In another bowl, beat egg whites with salt until they hold stiff peaks. Add one-quarter of the whites to the yolk mixture and fold them in gently but thoroughly. Pour the yolk mixture over the remaining whites and sprinkle with a mixture of nuts and ginger. Gently fold the mixture together until there are no traces of whites. Pour batter into pan and bake 25 minutes. When done, loosen the edges of the cake and turn out on a waxed paper sheet sprinkled with powdered sugar. Roll it up like a jelly roll and let it cool completely.

FILLING

1 teaspoon gelatin
3 tablespoons cold water

1 1/2 cups heavy cream
1/2 cup molasses

220

Put gelatin in cold water and heat over hot water until dissolved and liquid is clear. In a chilled bowl, whip heavy cream until it begins to thicken and gradually add the gelatin. Pour in the molasses and continue to whip the cream until stiff.

Unroll the cake, fill with two-thirds of the filling, and roll it up again. Put the remaining filling in a pastry bag fitted with a star tube and decorate the roll. Keep refrigerated until ready to serve.

BANANA WHIPPED CREAM ROLL

*1 unrolled Sponge Cake
  (page 215), cooled
2 cups heavy cream
½ cup sugar*

*1 teaspoon vanilla
4 sliced bananas
Chopped pecans*

Whip cream until thick, adding sugar and vanilla. Combine 1 cup whipped cream with bananas.

Spread the filling on the sponge cake. Roll up and ice with remaining whipped cream. If you want to make it more glamorous put the cream in a star-tipped pastry bag and run the cream over the top and sides of the roll. Sprinkle with pecans.

PRALINE NUT ROLL

PRALINE

1 cup filberts or unblanched
    almonds
1 cup sugar

¼ cup water
⅛ teaspoon cream of tartar

Preheat oven to 350°. Spread nuts in baking pan and roast for 25 minutes, or until lightly colored. When cooled, rub off the skins.

In a heavy skillet, cook sugar with water and cream of tartar—washing down with a brush dipped in cold water any undissolved sugar that clings to the sides of the pan—until the mixture is a light caramel. Add nuts and toss to coat them with caramel. Pour the mixture onto a buttered pan and let it cool.

Transfer the mixture to a board and chop it coarsely. Store the pieces in an airtight container at room temperature. Makes about 2 cups.

CAKE

5 eggs, separated
¾ cup sugar
1 cup ground toasted filberts
    (husks removed)
⅓ cup praline, crushed
3 tablespoons sifted
    all-purpose flour

1 teaspoon baking powder
1 teaspoon vanilla
¼ teaspoon salt
½ teaspoon cream of tartar

Preheat oven to 350°. Butter a jelly-roll pan 11″ x 16″ and line with waxed paper. Butter and lightly flour the paper.

In a bowl, beat egg yolks until frothy. Gradually add ½ cup sugar and continue to beat the mixture for several minutes, or until it ribbons when the beater is lifted. Stir in the filberts, praline powder, flour sifted with baking powder, and vanilla.

In another bowl, beat egg whites with clean beaters. Add salt and cream of tartar and beat until they hold soft peaks. Gradually beat in the remaining sugar, 1 tablespoon at a time, continuing to beat until stiff. Add one-quarter of the whites to the yolk mixture, folding them in gently but thoroughly. Pour the yolk mixture over the remaining whites and gently fold the mixture together until there are no traces of white.

Pour the batter into the pan and spread it evenly with a metal spatula. Bake for about 20 minutes, or until cake shrinks from sides of pan. Loosen the edges of the cake and invert on a tea towel sprinkled with powdered sugar. Let cool. Peel off the paper and roll up the cake. Let it cool completely.

FILLING

1 cup heavy cream   *1 teaspoon vanilla*
2 tablespoons powdered sugar

In a chilled bowl, beat heavy cream until it thickens. Beat in the powdered sugar and vanilla. Continue to beat the cream until it holds stiff peaks.

Unroll the cake and spread with the whipped cream.

FROSTING

½ cup brown sugar
¼ cup heavy cream
3 tablespoons sweet butter

7 tablespoons powdered sugar
¼ cup praline, crushed

In a small saucepan, combine brown sugar, cream, and butter. Bring the mixture to a boil and cook over moderate heat, stirring for 2 minutes. Let it cool to lukewarm. Beat in the powdered sugar.

With a spatula, spread the frosting over the roll and garnish with the praline. Transfer the roll to a serving tray.

PASTRIES

BASIC SWEET DOUGH

This dough has many possibilities. This amount of dough makes two dozen schnecken (pecan rolls). This amount of dough also makes two dozen cinnamon rolls. These rolls freeze very well—or you can give them to some of your friends or you can cut the recipe in half.

1 quart milk
6 squares or 3 ounces yeast,
*   powdered or in cake form*
2 cups sugar

14 cups all-purpose flour
1 tablespoon salt
1 pound sweet butter
12 egg yolks

Scald milk and cool to lukewarm. Add yeast, 1 cup sugar and 2 cups flour (this is your sponge). Let it rise about 30 minutes.

In a large bowl, sift in the rest of the flour, salt, and remaining sugar. With your fingertips, work butter into the dry ingredients, then add yolks and the yeast sponge. Stir, then work with your hands until quite thick. Knead the dough on a board sprinkled with flour until it becomes smooth and elastic. (You may have to add more flour to make for easier handling.) Cover and let rise about 1 to 1½ hours. Punch down and knead again for a few minutes. Cover and let rise again for 30 minutes.

BUTTERFLIES

1 recipe Basic Sweet Dough
(page 227)
¼ cup melted sweet butter

1 tablespoon cinnamon
½ cup sugar
1 cup ground nuts (optional)

Make basic sweet dough. Grease a baking sheet. Roll a sheet of dough in a rectangle ½" thick and sprinkle with melted butter, cinnamon, sugar, and ground nuts. Roll up like a jelly roll. Cut in 1" wide pieces. Make a cut in the center of each roll, then turn the edges back. Place on baking sheet and let rise for 30 minutes. Bake in 350° oven for about 40 minutes.

SCHNECKEN (PECAN ROLLS)

While these are baking, they sometimes leak a little of the syrup. To avoid a lot of extra work, place a foil oven liner under each pan of schnecken.

GLAZE

4 ounces sweet butter
½ pound light brown sugar

4 tablespoons light corn syrup
Pecan halves

Preheat oven to 350°. In a saucepan, place butter, sugar, and corn syrup. Cook over moderate heat for about 10 minutes. Put 1 tablespoon of this mixture into each cup of 2 muffin pans. Top with 5 or 6 halves of pecans.

DOUGH

1 recipe Basic Sweet Dough	*2 tablespoons cinnamon*
(page 227)	*1 cup sugar*
½ cup melted sweet butter	*1 cup pecan pieces*

Prepare basic sweet dough. Roll half of the dough into a sheet ½" thick. Sprinkle liberally with melted butter, cinnamon, sugar, and pecans. Roll up tight and cut into 1" wide slices.

Place each slice of dough on top of the glazed cups of the muffin pans and let rise for 1 hour. Bake for about 45 minutes. When the pan on the top shelf browns, reverse pans by putting bottom on top and vice versa. As soon as rolls are baked, remove from oven, cover the top with oven liner and turn upside down. Wait 1 minute and remove muffin pans.

CINNAMON ROLLS

½ recipe Basic Sweet Dough	*1 tablespoon cinnamon*
(page 227)	*½ cup sugar*
¼ cup melted sweet butter	

Make basic sweet dough. Grease a baking sheet. Roll the dough into a rectangular sheet ½" thick. Sprinkle liberally with melted butter, cinnamon, and sugar. Roll tightly like a jelly roll and cut into 1" thick slices. Place about 1" apart on baking sheet. Let rise for 1 hour and bake in 350° oven for about 45 minutes. Remove from oven.

ICING

2 cups powdered sugar
1 teaspoon vanilla

About ¼ cup hot water

Mix all ingredients until smooth.
Ice the rolls while they are hot.

TWISTED NUT ROLLS

NUT FILLING

⅓ cup sweet butter
1 cup powdered sugar

1 cup ground almonds or pecans

Cream butter. Blend in sugar thoroughly. Add nuts.

DOUGH

2 cakes yeast or 2 packages
   dry yeast
¼ cup lukewarm water
⅓ cup sweet butter
¾ cup milk, scalded

⅓ cup sugar
2 teaspoons salt
2 teaspoons grated orange rind
2 unbeaten eggs
4 to 4½ cups all-purpose flour

Soften yeast in water. Combine butter and hot milk in a large bowl. Stir until butter melts. Cool and add ⅓ cup sugar, salt, orange rind, eggs, and yeast mixture. Gradually add flour to form a stiff dough. Mix thoroughly and cover. Let stand 30 minutes.

Roll out the dough on a floured board to a 22″ x 12″ rectangle. Spread the filling on half of the dough along the 22″ side. Fold the other half over the filling. Cut into 1″ strips crosswise and twist each strip 4 or 5 times. Hold one end of each strip down on a baking sheet for the center of the roll and curl the strip around the center, tucking the other end under. Cover with a towel and let rise until light and doubled in size, 45 minutes to 1 hour. Bake in 375° oven for 15 minutes, or until golden brown.

GLAZE

¼ cup orange juice   *3 tablespoons sugar*

Combine orange juice and sugar.

Brush top of rolls with the glaze and bake 5 minutes longer, or until deep golden brown. Remove from baking sheet immediately.

ALMOND NUT ROLLS

½ recipe Basic Sweet Dough
   (page 227)
¼ cup melted butter

½ cup sugar
1 tablespoon cinnamon
1 cup ground toasted almonds

Grease cookie sheet. Make basic sweet dough. Roll dough to ½" thickness, then sprinkle with melted butter, sugar, cinnamon, and almonds. Roll up and cut into 1" slices and place on cookie sheet 1" apart to rise for about 1 hour. Bake in 350° oven for about 45 minutes. Remove from oven and sprinkle with powdered sugar.

DIAMOND CRISPS

3 cups all-purpose flour
1 cup sweet butter
1 cake of yeast or 1 package
   dry yeast
¼ cup warm water

½ cup sweetened condensed milk
2 egg whites
¼ cup sugar
1 teaspoon cinnamon
½ cup any nuts you like, ground

With fingertips, rub the flour and butter until the mixture resembles coarse crumbs. In a small bowl, combine yeast and warm water and let stand until dissolved. Stir in the milk. Gradually add liquid to flour-butter mixture, stirring with a wooden spoon until the dough forms a ball. Cover and refrigerate for about 2 hours.

Divide dough in half. On a heavily floured board, pat each ball of dough and roll into a ⅛″ thick 10″ x 18″ rectangle. Cut 5 lengthwise strips 2″ wide, then starting from points 3″ apart on the long edge, cut on a slant to make diamond shapes.

Preheat over to 350°. Lightly grease a baking sheet. Use a spatula to lift the pieces of dough and arrange on a baking sheet. Brush with beaten egg whites and sprinkle with sugar, cinnamon, and nuts. Let rise uncovered for 10 minutes. Bake for about 15 minutes.

VIENNESE DOUGHNUTS

These are sort of cakey and delicate. A nice change from the regular doughnut.

DOUGHNUTS

2 cakes yeast
½ cup milk
4¾ cups pastry flour
1 cup sugar
6 tablespoons sweet butter
3 egg yolks

3 ounces rum
1 teaspoon vanilla
½ teaspoon salt
Grated rind of 1 lemon
Fat for deep frying

Dissolve yeast in a little of the warm milk. Add one-third of the flour to form yeast sponge. Let rise well. Meanwhile, cream sugar, butter, egg yolks, rum, vanilla, salt, and lemon rind. Add sponge and the balance of the flour plus any remaining milk. Knead well until the dough is soft and silky. Let rise until double in bulk, then roll until ½" thick. Cut with a doughnut cutter and let rise for about 30 minutes.

If you have a regular deep French fryer, that's fine. If not, use your electric skillet or a good heavy plain skillet. Heat shortening about 3" deep to 380° and fry the doughnuts a few at a time until light and brown on one side. Turn and finish frying on other side. Drain on heavy brown paper and let cool. When properly fried, doughnuts will show a white ring around the center.

ICING

1 cup confectioners' sugar *1 teaspoon vanilla*
About 4 tablespoons hot water

Beat until smooth and ice the doughnuts.

PUFFED DOUGHNUTS

These really don't belong in the yeast cake section, but they are good and puffy.

1⅛ cups milk *Pinch of salt*
½ cup sweet butter *1¼ cups sifted all-purpose flour*
1 tablespoon sugar *6 eggs*

In a large skillet (do not use an enamel pan), simmer milk, butter, sugar, and salt, until the butter is just melted. Remove the pan from heat and add flour all at once, mixing it in quickly. Cook again, stirring the dough constantly for 5 to 8 minutes. (The dough must continue to cook even after it leaves the sides of the pan.)

Turn the dough into a bowl, let it cool slightly and beat in the eggs, one at a time, mixing thoroughly. Using the largest fluted tube of a pastry bag, pipe the dough in rounds onto well-buttered heavy paper. Carefully turn the paper over and drop each doughnut into deep fat, heated to 370°. Fry the rounds for 6 to 8 minutes. Do not cook too many doughnuts at one time. They will turn themselves over as soon as one side is done. Skim them off with a slotted spoon. Sprinkle with powdered sugar and drain on paper toweling.

DANISH PASTRY

This recipe for Danish rolls may sound complicated, but as you work with it you will see how simple it really is and the result will be well worth it, and will please you. Good luck!

4 yeast cakes, or 4 packages
   dry yeast
¼ cup warm water
½ cup plus 2 tablespoons
   sugar
3 cups sweet butter

7½ cups all-purpose flour
½ teaspoon salt
2 whole eggs
4 egg yolks
2½ cups milk

Dissolve the yeast in the warm water, to which 2 tablespoons sugar have been added. Set aside. Cream butter with ⅔ cup flour and form into a large flat square. Wrap in foil and let harden in refrigerator for about 1 hour.

Sift the remaining flour in a large bowl. Add remaining sugar, salt, eggs, egg yolks, yeast mixture, and cold milk. Beat with a wooden spoon until smooth and glossy, then knead the dough on a floured board until no longer sticky. Let rest for about 1 hour.

Roll the dough into a large rectangle. Place a square of cold butter in the center of the dough. Fold one side of the dough over the butter and put the other side over the top, making three layers. Turn the dough and roll out to a rectangle. Repeat the whole process. Refrigerate for 1 hour and then repeat the process of rolling and folding the dough and turning it—do this six times. If the butter gets too soft, stop rolling and refrigerate the dough for about 1 hour so that it will harden. Place the dough in the refrigerator for about 2 hours or overnight if you wish.

Next morning, work with half of the dough at a time, leaving the unused portion in the refrigerator. Roll out to about ½″ thickness, cut in strips and roll each strip round and round to form individual rolls. This amount of dough makes about 2 dozen rolls about 3″ wide. Let rise in refrigerator. Bake in 400° oven for 10 minutes. Reduce heat to 375° and finish baking—total baking time, about 25 minutes.

ICING

2 cups powdered sugar   *1 teaspoon vanilla*
½ cup hot water

Stir ingredients. If too thin, add more sugar. If too thick, add water.
Spread the icing on top of the hot rolls.

DANISH NUT PASTRIES

1 recipe Danish Pastry (page 235)

Chill dough for about 1 hour. Remove from refrigerator and roll out into a large rectangle ½″ thick.

FILLING

2 cups ground nuts
1 cup sugar
½ cup cookie or cake crumbs

4 tablespoons sweet butter,
softened
1 teaspoon cinnamon

Mix all ingredients thoroughly.

Sprinkle the filling over the entire surface of the rectangle of dough. Roll up like a jelly roll and place half of the roll in a greased bread pan and the other half on a greased baking sheet. Cut at 2″ intervals and turn each to form a circle. Let rest for 30 minutes, then bake in 375° oven for about 45 minutes.

ICING

1 cup powdered sugar
1 teaspoon vanilla

4 tablespoons water

Mix thoroughly.

Ice the top of the hot rolls and sprinkle with chopped nuts if you like.

VIENNESE COFFEE CAKE

4 yeast cakes or 4 packages
   dry yeast
½ cup warm water
1½ cups plus 2 tablespoons
   sugar
1 pound butter
8 eggs, separated
1½ cups warm milk

1 tablespoon rum or orange
   flavoring
8 cups all-purpose flour
1 teaspoon salt
2 cups ground nuts
1 cup blanched almonds
2 tablespoons light corn syrup

Dissolve the yeast in the warm water to which you have added 2 tablespoons sugar. Cream the butter, add 1 cup sugar, and beat in the yolks one by one. Add yeast mixture, warm milk, and flavoring, then add the flour mixed with salt. Beat until the dough leaves the sides of the bowl. Cover and put in the refrigerator overnight. (You'll notice that I don't recommend kneading this dough. If the dough is still a little sticky, don't worry about it—in the morning it will be solid.)

Remove from refrigerator. Cut in half and put one half back in the refrigerator until ready to use. Beat egg whites until stiff. Very gradually add remaining sugar, then fold in the nuts. Roll each half of the dough until very thin. Spread with the filling and roll up like a jelly roll. Liberally butter a Bundt kuchen pan, sprinkle with blanched almonds, and pour corn syrup over them. Put the rolled dough on top and let rise for about 2 hours. Bake in 350° oven for 50 minutes to 1 hour. When nicely browned, remove from oven and turn out of pan at once. Let cool on a cake rack.

You may use the remaining dough you have stored in your refrigerator for the recipes that follow.

COFFEE CAKE WITH COTTAGE CHEESE FILLING

¼ *recipe Basic Sweet Dough*
   (page 227)
¼ *cup melted butter*

1 *tablespoon cinnamon*
½ *cup sugar*

Make basic sweet dough. Roll out to ½″ thickness, sprinkle with melted butter, cinnamon, and sugar.

CHEESE FILLING

1 *pound strained cottage*
   cheese
4 *egg yolks*
½ *cup sugar*

4 *tablespoons golden raisins*
Grated rind of 1 lemon
1 *teaspoon vanilla*
3 *tablespoons sour cream*

Mix all ingredients until smooth.

Put the mixture on one end of the sheet of dough. Roll up like a jelly roll and place on a greased baking sheet. Let rise for 30 minutes and bake in 350° oven for about 45 minutes.

ALMOND RAISIN RING

This cake freezes very well.

1¼ cups milk	2 eggs
¾ cup sweet butter	1 teaspoon grated orange rind
¾ cup sugar	4 cups all-purpose flour
1 teaspoon salt	4 tablespoons blanched almonds
2 cakes yeast or 2 packages	2 tablespoons light corn syrup
dry yeast	1 cup raisins, soaked in 2
¼ cup warm water	tablespoons cognac

Scald milk, add butter, and stir in sugar and salt until dissolved. Soften yeast in lukewarm water and let stand for 10 minutes.

Put the milk mixture in the large bowl of an electric mixer. Add eggs, yeast mixture, and orange rind. On low speed, beat in 3 cups flour until smooth. Add remaining flour and beat well. Cover the bowl and let the dough rise for about 1½ hours, or until triple in bulk.

Butter a 10" tube or Bundt pan, sprinkle liberally with the blanched almonds, and pour 2 tablespoons light corn syrup over them.

Stir the dough and add raisins. Beat vigorously with a heavy spoon for a few minutes and spoon into the pan. Cover and let rise for about 35 minutes, or until double in bulk. Bake in lower part of oven, heated to 350°, for about 45 minutes. Let the cake rest in the pan for 2 minutes and turn out onto a platter.

APPLE SLICES

4 cups cake flour
½ teaspoon salt
1 cup plus 6 tablespoons sugar
1 cup sweet butter
4 eggs, separated
½ cup sour cream

1 tablespoon bread crumbs
3 pounds greening apples,
 peeled and chopped
Grated rind of 1 orange
1 teaspoon cinnamon

Mix flour with salt and 4 tablespoons sugar. Cut in the cold butter with your fingertips. Beat yolks, mix with sour cream, and add to butter-flour mixture, stirring well. Form the dough into a ball. Wrap in waxed paper and refrigerate for 4 hours.

Preheat oven to 375°. Thoroughly grease and flour a 14″ x 16″ sheet pan.

Cut chilled dough into 4 parts. Roll out each piece to fit the pan. (It is easier to use 2 parts for the bottom and 2 parts for the top. Use hands freely to patch the dough if necessary.) Sprinkle bottom crust with crumbs and spread with apples, orange rind, 1 cup sugar, and cinnamon. Cover with remaining dough and seal the edges. Brush the top with slightly beaten egg whites and sprinkle with remaining sugar. Bake for about 50 minutes, or until brown and crisp-looking.

FROSTING

¾ cup powdered sugar
1 teaspoon vanilla

2 tablespoons hot cream

Mix and drizzle over the hot cake. Tilt the pan so that the frosting runs. When the cake is cool, cut into slices.

FRUIT TORTE

DOUGH

2 cakes yeast or 2 packages
   dry yeast
½ cup lukewarm water
1½ cups sweet butter,
   softened

4 cups all-purpose flour
4 egg yolks
2 tablespoons sugar
½ cup sour cream

Dissolve yeast in water. Cream the butter, add 1 cup flour and blend well. Add egg yolks and beat thoroughly. Add yeast, sugar, and sour cream, and beat in the remaining flour. Turn out onto a floured pastry cloth and knead until smooth. Let dough stand for about 30 minutes. Divide into three parts. Roll one portion to fit a 13″ x 9″ x 2″ pan and place it in the pan.

FILLING

1½ cups chopped pecans
1¼ cups sugar
1 teaspoon cinnamon
¼ cup sweet butter, softened

1 cup chopped fresh apples or
   Apricot Purée (page 125)
4 egg whites

Blend 1 cup nuts with ¾ cup sugar, cinnamon, and butter until crumbly.

Sprinkle the nut mixture over the dough. Roll out the second portion of dough to the same size and place over the nut mixture. Gently spread the fruit filling over the dough. Roll out the third portion to the same size and cover the fruit filling. Bake for 45 minutes. Remove from oven. Beat egg whites until stiff. Add remaining sugar gradually and beat until stiff. Spread over the top layer and sprinkle with remaining nuts. Return to oven and bake for 15 minutes longer. Cut into small squares to serve.

INDEX